CRETE

|CONDENSED|

 jeanne oliver

LONELY PLANET PUBLICATIONS
Melbourne • Oakland • London • Paris

contents

Lonely Planet Condensed – Crete
1st edition – April 2000

Published by
Lonely Planet Publications Pty Ltd
A.C.N. 005 607 983
192 Burwood Rd, Hawthorn,
Victoria 3122, Australia

Lonely Planet Offices
Australia PO Box 617, Hawthorn, VIC 3122
USA 150 Linden St, Oakland, CA 94607
UK 10a Spring Place, London NW5 3BH
France 1 rue du Dahomey, 75011 Paris

Photographs
Most of the images in this guide are
available for licensing from Lonely Planet
Images. email: lpi@lonelyplanet.com.au

Front cover photographs
Top: Fishing boats, Rethymno
    (Jon Davison)
Bottom: A bountiful catch
    (Neil Setchfield)

ISBN 1 86450 042 5

text & maps © Lonely Planet 2000
photos © photographers as indicated 2000

Printed by The Bookmaker Pty Ltd
Printed in China

FACTS ABOUT CRETE   5

History   6
   The Minoans   6
   Roman & Byzantine Crete   7
   Venetian Crete   7
   Turkish Crete   8
   Union with Greece   8
   War & Occupation   9
   Crete Today   9
Geography   10
Environment   10
Government & Politics   11
Economy   12
Society & Culture   12
   Dos & Don'ts   13
Arts   14

HIGHLIGHTS   15

Archaeological Museum,
   Iraklio   16
Argiroupolis   18
Elafonisi Beach   19
Frangokastello   20
Gortyn   21
Knossos   22
Lassithi Plateau   24
Hania's Old Quarter   26
Moni Preveli & Preveli Beach   27
Moni Toplou   28
Phaestos   29
Rethymno's Old Quarter   30
Samaria Gorge   31
Sitia   32
Zakros Palace & Kato Zakros   33
Crete Lowlights   34

SIGHTS & ACTIVITIES   35

Agios Nikolaos   35
Hania   36
Ierapetra   38
Imbros Gorge   39
Iraklio   40
Kritsa   42
Rethymno   43

Beaches   44
Ancient Sites   46
Venetian & Byzantine
   Legacies   48
Crete for Children   49
Off the Beaten Track   50
Quirky Crete   51
Keeping Fit   53
   Cycling & Mountain Biking   53
   Gyms   53
   Hiking   54
   Horse Riding   54
   Snorkelling & Diving   54
   Swimming   55
   Water Sports   55

OUT & ABOUT   56

Walking Tours   57
Driving Tours   64
Organised Tours   66

SHOPPING   68

   VAT Refund   69
   Opening Hours   69
Agios Nikolaos   70
Hania   71
Iraklio   73
Rethymno   74
Around Crete   75

PLACES TO EAT   76

Agios Nikolaos   77
Hania   79
Iraklio   81
Rethymno   84
Around Crete   86
   West   86
   Central   86
   East   87
Internet Cafes   87

ENTERTAINMENT   88

What's On   89
Agios Nikolaos   90

Hania   91
Iraklio   93
Rethymno   95
Around Crete   96

PLACES TO STAY   97

Agios Nikolaos   98
Hania   99
Iraklio   101
Rethymno   103
Around Crete   105

FACTS FOR THE VISITOR

Pre-Departure   108
Arrival & Departure   109
Getting Around   110
Practical Information   113

INDEX   124

SIGHTS INDEX   128

MAP INDEX

Walking Tours
Hania's Old Quarter   57
Iraklio Stroll   59
Samaria Gorge Hike   61
Lassithi Plateau Walk   62
Paleohora-Sougia   63

Driving Tours
Hania to the Samaria
   Gorge   64
Agios Nikolaos to Sitia   65

Front Cover Gatefold
Map 1 – Iraklio
Map 2 – Crete

Back Cover Gatefold
Map 3 – Agios Nikolaos
Map 4 – Rethymno
Map 5 – Hania

how to use this book

KEY TO SYMBOLS

⊠	address	⌚	opening hours
☎	telephone number	⑤	cost, entry charge
𝒆	email/web site address	♿	wheelchair access
🚌	nearest bus route	⚲	child-friendly
⚓	nearest ferry wharf	✗	on-site or nearby eatery
🚗	car access	**V**	vegetarian, or with a good
①	tourist information		vegetarian selection

COLOUR-CODING

Each chapter has a different colour code which is reflected on the maps for quick reference.

MAPS & GRID REFERENCES

The fold-out maps on the front and back covers are numbered from 1 to 5. All sights and venues in the text have map references which indicate where to find them, eg (3, H4) means Map 3, grid reference H4. When a map reference appears immediately after a name, the sight is labelled on the map; when it appears after an address (eg with some restaurants, hotels etc), only the street is marked.

PRICES

Multiple prices, separated by a backslash (eg $14/10), indicate adult/concession entry charges or costs. Concession prices include child, pensioner and/or student discounts.

WARNING & REQUEST

Things change – prices go up, schedules change, good places go bad and bad places improve or go bankrupt. So, if you find things better or worse, recently opened or long since closed, please tell us and help make the next edition even more accurate and useful. Everyone who writes to us will find their name and possibly excerpts from their correspondence in one of our publications (let us know if you *don't* want your letter published or your name acknowledged). They will also receive the latest issue of *Planet Talk*, our quarterly printed newsletter, or *Comet*, our monthly email newsletter. Subscriptions to both newsletters are free. The very best contributions will be rewarded with a free guidebook.

Send all correspondence to the Lonely Planet office closest to you (see p. 123).

Lonely Planet books provide independent advice. Lonely Planet does not accept advertising in guidebooks, nor payment in exchange for listing or endorsing any place or business. Lonely Planet writers do not accept discounts or payments in exchange for positive coverage of any sort.

facts about crete

The largest and southernmost Greek island, Crete is a land of exhilarating contrasts – mountains and sea, cities and pastures, ancient ruins and sleek resorts. It's easy for visitors to remain on the seductive rim of beaches and coves – the sun is always shining and the Mediterranean is warm, clear and inviting. Venture into the interior, however, and the languid coastal panorama gives way to a harsh mountainous landscape of steep gorges blanketed with wildflowers and aromatic herbs. It is here that the back-breaking work of shepherding, olive-growing and farming continues as it has for centuries.

Away from the beaches and resorts, Crete's colourful history comes alive. Zeus, the father of Greek mythology, was, according to legend, born and raised in the island's caves. A wealth of Minoan ruins conjure up a civilisation that vanished over 3000 years ago. Crete's former Venetian overlords built fortresses that still dominate coastal cities. Cretans and Turks battled furiously around remote monasteries, pirates staged raids from offshore islets, and scars from WWII's famous Battle of Crete are still visible around the island.

The songs, dances, poetry and cuisine that survived centuries of struggle are the chief joy of a visit to Crete. In village tavernas, at festivals and weddings, you'll see Cretans feasting on their own robust dishes and cutting loose to traditional Cretan folk songs.

Cretans say that visitors to their island cry twice – first when they come and then when they leave. Overdevelopment along the northern coast can make a poor first impression but it doesn't take long to unearth the splendours of this fascinating island. Hike through a gorge, poke around an archaeological site, take a harbourside walk at sunset, spend an evening listening to Cretan songs in a taverna. Don't cry when you leave – just plan your next trip back.

Hania: it wouldn't be a Cretan city without a harbourside promenade

HISTORY
The Minoans

Although the island has been inhabited since Neolithic times (7000-3000BC), it was the Minoans who assumed the starring role in prehistoric Crete from 3000 to 1400BC. Excavations at the palaces of Knossos, Phaestos, Malia and Zakros have revealed a prosperous, artistic and well-functioning society that was the most highly developed in Bronze Age Europe. Spiritual life was organised around the worship of a mother goddess and material well-being was assured by a constant flow of trade with Egypt and Asia Minor. The celebrated frescoes in the Archaeological Museum of Iraklio depict lithe, handsome people that delighted in song, dance, games, feasting and hunting.

Minoan culture came to an abrupt halt around 1450BC, for reasons that have not yet been fully unravelled. After an earthquake circa 1700BC destroyed all 4 palaces, the Minoans rebuilt and their civilisation reached new heights. Yet in a great cataclysm not even 3 centuries later, the palaces (except Knossos) and numerous smaller settlements were smashed to bits and burned. Some archaeologists believe that the destruction was due to the eruption of a volcano in nearby Santorini, while others believe that the damage was caused by invading Mycenaeans eager to grab the Minoans' maritime commerce.

Discovering the Minoans

Sir Arthur Evans was an archaeologist, journalist and adventurer who began his dig at Knossos in 1900 upon a hunch and soon uncovered the remains of an immense palace dating from 1700BC. Evans named the civilisation Minoan after King Minos, the legendary leader of a great naval power whose capital was the Palace of Knossos. Although he was criticised for an overly imaginative renovation of the site, Evans' rebuilt columns and supports undoubtedly make the palace more visitor-friendly. Evans spent about £250,000 of his personal fortune over 30 years to unearth the jewellery, pottery, religious objects and frescoes that depict Minoan society. Most of the treasured objects are on display in the Archaeological Museum in Iraklio.

Yesterday's larder: a storehouse in the Minoan palace at Phaestos

Roman & Byzantine Crete

The Mycenaeans were followed by the warlike Dorians, and by 67BC Crete had fallen to the Romans. Although Roman occupation did not prompt any artistic accomplishments, various improvement projects left the island with roads, bridges and aqueducts. When the Roman Empire divided in 395AD, Crete, along with the rest of Greece, became part of the Byzantine Empire.

During the 5th and 6th centuries scores of churches were built, indicating that the island remained comparatively wealthy from the export of its agricultural products. The Arab occupation of 824-961 was marked by economic decline and the island became more known for its piracy than its farming. When the Byzantine Empire finally recovered Crete in 961, churches and fortifications were built and 12 noble families (*Arhontopouli*) were established as a bulwark of Christianity. They later became powerful voices of rebellion against Venetian rule.

Venetian Crete

After the sacking of Constantinople in 1204, Crete was sold to the Republic of Venice. It remained under Venetian rule for over 4 centuries (1204-1669). The first centuries of Venetian rule were marked by oppressive taxation and ruthless economic exploitation, which sparked a series of rebellions that eventually forced concessions from the republic. By the 15th century the Cretan and Venetian communities reached an

Mythical Crete

In the beginning there was Cronus, master of the universe, who was married to Rhea. Having been warned that one of his children would overthrow him, he decided to eat all his progeny. When Rhea was about to give birth to Zeus she fed her husband a stone wrapped in swaddling cloth and ran off to the Dikteon cave on the Lassithi plateau to give birth. The young god eventually toppled Cronus and became king of the gods.

Although married to his sister Hera, Zeus fell in love with Europa and had 3 children with her on Crete. One of their children was the legendary Minos who became King of Crete. Minos married Pasiphae, who developed an uncontrollable lust for a bull. The result of this unusual passion was the Minotaur, a monster with the body of a man and the head of a bull. Seeking to hide his wife's disgrace, Minos had a labyrinth built for the Minotaur under the Palace of Knossos.

Eventually Theseus of Athens killed the Minotaur with the aid of Minos' daughter, Ariadne, who showed him how to use a ball of thread to escape the labyrinth. When Minos later learned that Daedalus had a role in his wife's adultery, he ordered that Daedalus and his son, Icarus, be put to death. Daedalus escaped the island by outfitting himself and Icarus with wings made of wax, but Icarus flew too close to the sun, the wax melted and he fell into the sea.

Paul Hellander

Icarus takes the plunge

The Venetian Arsenal in Hania

uneasy compromise that allowed Cretan cultural and economic life to flourish.

As the Turks closed in around Constantinople in the mid-15th century, Byzantine scholars and intellectuals fled to Crete and set up schools, reviving Byzantine and Greek culture. At the same time many Cretans went to Italy for their education and returned with the invigorating influences of the Italian Renaissance. Poetry and drama flourished and the 'Cretan School' of icon painting, combining Byzantine and Venetian elements, developed in the 16th and 17th centuries. In the midst of this artistic ferment, the painter Domeniko Theotokopoulos was born in Iraklio in 1541. He studied in Italy under Titian and later moved to Spain where he became known as El Greco (p. 14).

Turkish Crete

Venice fell into decline in the 17th century and the Ottoman Turks moved quickly to secure Venetian colonies. By 1648 the Turks had occupied the entire island except Iraklio which they besieged for 21 years. The Cretan artistic renaissance flickered out as libraries were destroyed and the intelligentsia fled the island. Taxed into penury and harassed by the arbitrary rule of the Janissaries (p. 37), many Cretans converted to Islam to escape the harshest effects of Ottoman rule. The most serious rebellion was launched in Sfakia in 1770 but Turkish reprisals were severe and the spirit of insurrection lay dormant until the Greek struggle for independence in 1821 prompted another failed attempt to throw off the Ottoman yoke.

The 1830 Protocol of London recognised Greek independence but handed Crete over to Egypt under whose control it remained for 10 years until the Great Powers gave it back to the Ottomans. The incessant turmoil on the island and reports of Turkish atrocities eventually turned European public opinion in favour of Cretan self-rule. In 1898 the Great Powers granted the island autonomy and appointed Prince George, son of the Greek king, as governor.

Union with Greece

Union with its cultural brethren in Greece remained an unquenchable desire in Crete. A new movement coalesced around the Cretan Eleftherios Venizelos, who formed a rival government seeking union with Greece. The

Cretan Assembly unilaterally declared union with Greece in 1908 but the Greek government refused to allow Cretan deputies to sit in the Greek Parliament. Even though Venizelos had become Greek Prime Minister, Greece remained fearful of antagonising Turkey and the Great Powers. Only after Turkey's defeat in the First Balkan War was the union of Crete and Greece formally implemented in 1913. The following decades were good for Crete as literacy levels climbed and medical care improved.

War & Occupation

Planning to use the island as an airbase in the Mediterranean, the Germans staged an airborne landing on Crete in 1941. The local population mounted a fierce defence and casualties were heavy on both sides before the Germans prevailed 10 days later. A strong resistance movement helped stranded British, Australian and New Zealand forces withdraw from the island. German reprisals against the civilian population were heavy and many mountain villages were bombed 'off the map'.

Nikos Kazantzakis

Greece's best-known writer since Homer, Nikos Kazantzakis (1883-1957) was born in Iraklio amid the last spasms of Crete's struggle for independence from the Turks. Educated in Athens and abroad, Kazantzakis produced books on philosophy and travel, novels, poetry, plays, screenplays, translations and hundreds of articles. In Greece, he's best known for *The Odyssey*, a sequel to Homer's original; *Freedom or Death*, which deals with the Turkish occupation; and his translations of literary classics. His international fame rests upon *Zorba the Greek* and *The Last Temptation of Christ* which were made into films. His tomb in Iraklio is inscribed with his quotation: 'I hope for nothing. I fear nothing. I am free.'

Crete Today

Having avoided the postwar civil war that ravaged the rest of Greece, Crete moved rapidly into a period of unprecedented economic development largely based upon agriculture and tourism. Union with Greece has brought the island the advantages of EU membership and subsidies as well as a much-improved infrastructure. Crete is now one of the most prosperous regions in Greece. Wealth has in no way diminished the Cretans' pride in their unique culture, however. The traditional songs, dances, food and dress are kept alive and on display, especially at weddings and local festivals.

Neil Setchfield

Proud of the old ways, pragmatic about the new

GEOGRAPHY

Crete is the largest island in the Greek archipelago, with an area of 8335 sq km. It is 250km long, about 60km at its widest point and 12km at its narrowest. Three major mountain groups define the rugged interior: the White Mountains (Lefka Ori) in the west, Mount Ida (Psiloritis) in the centre and the Lassithi Mountains in the east. The White Mountains are known for their spectacular gorges, such as the Samaria, as well as for the snow that lingers on the peaks well into spring. Psiloritis contains hundreds of caves and the Rouva forest on the southern slopes. The Lassithi Mountains have the famous Lassithi plateau and Mt Dikti, whose southern slopes preserve an example of the magnificent forests that once blanketed the island. Steep mountains in the south and gently sloping mountains in the north border the 1046km coastline.

Loggerhead Turtles

Caretta Caretta is the Latin name for the loggerhead sea turtle that has been nesting on Crete since the days of the dinosaurs. The beaches of Rethymno, Hania and the Messara Gulf in the south can host 500 to 800 nests each summer. Sadly, beachfront development has seriously disturbed the nesting habits of this ancient species. Because they are so vulnerable on land, the females are frightened by objects on the beach at night and can refuse to lay eggs. When the hatchlings emerge at night they find the sea by the reflection of moon and starlight but are easily disoriented by tavern lights.

The Sea Turtle Protection Society of Greece has the following advice for visitors:

- Leave beaches clear at night during the May-October nesting season
- Remove umbrellas and lounge chairs at night
- Don't touch baby turtles on their way to the sea
- Urge hotel and tavern owners to shade their lights when necessary
- Dispose of rubbish properly; plastic bags kill turtles because they mistake them for a jellyfish dinner.

A living dinosaur: the loggerhead turtle

Lee Foster

ENVIRONMENT

Crete has clean air and water, especially outside the major cities, but the flora and fauna are under pressure. Olive cultivation, firewood gathering, shipbuilding, uncontrolled livestock breeding and arson over the centuries have laid waste to the island's forests. The nesting grounds of the loggerhead sea turtle are on the same sandy beaches that tourists prize. Marine life has suffered from the local custom of fishing with dynamite, and overdevelopment of the north coast is chasing away migratory birds.

As tourism on Crete has ballooned over the past 2 decades, the island has had to cope with increasing demands for electricity. Although the power had long been provided by fossil fuels, Greenpeace launched a major campaign in 1996 and persuaded the Greek

From idyllic beaches to soaring mountain ranges, Crete has it all

government to help build the world's largest solar-power plant on Crete. When completed in 2003, the plant will provide 50MW of solar power, which is enough power for almost 100,000 people. It is expected that the cost of electricity will be low enough to make the Crete installation a prototype for other solar-power projects in the Mediterranean.

GOVERNMENT & POLITICS

Greece is a parliamentary republic with a president as head of state. It is divided into 51 prefectures, of which Crete contains four: Lassithi, Iraklio, Rethymno and Hania. The island's capital (and Greece's fifth-largest city) is Iraklio, with a population of 127,600. Hania, the island's capital until 1971, considers itself the historical heart of the island and Rethymno claims to be its cultural centre. Rivalries between the prefectures are strong as each competes for investment, tourism and, more recently, distribution of the island's water supply.

Centuries of battling foreign occupiers have left the island with a stubbornly independent streak that sometimes leads to clashes with Athens. NATO bases on the island are a sore point with the local population who would like to see them removed despite foreign-policy commitments by the national government. National laws that conflict with local customs are simply disregarded. Guns are strictly regulated in Greece but nearly every household in Crete has at least one illegal firearm and many harbour small arsenals.

Politically, the island is predominantly left-of-centre, with the socialist PASOK party repeatedly outdrawing the conservative ND or New Democracy party in local and national elections. Extremists on both the right and left have little support.

ECONOMY

Agriculture and tourism are the twin engines of the Cretan economy. The unemployment rate of 5.5% is less than half the national rate. Olives, olive oil, sultana raisins, wine, vegetables and fruit are exported. Although fewer people are working in agriculture than in the postwar period, improvements in roads and better techniques are allowing the output to remain the same or increase. Tourism has expanded to the point where it constitutes two-thirds of the Gross Regional Product of Crete and provides employment to 40% of the island's workforce. The labour-intensive tourism sector draws seasonal workers from mainland Greece, the EU and eastern Europe to work in hotels, restaurants, shops and bars.

did you know?
- Crete has a population of 540,000
- Over 2 million tourists visit Crete each year
- 80% of visitors are on package tours
- The annual turnover from tourism is about US$1.5 billion
- Crete has 25 million olive trees
- A one-bedroom house in Hania's Old Town will put you back about 20,000,000 dr (approx US$73,000)
- 3500 sq km of land is devoted to agriculture

Neil Setchfield

Neil Setchfield

Olives and tourists are both essential to Crete's economy

SOCIETY & CULTURE

Proud, patriotic, hospitable and religious, today's Cretans retain a strong connection to their ancestors, which is apparent as soon as you leave the major tourist centres. Mountain villages are repositories of traditional culture and you'll find that most older women and many men are still clad in black. During weddings and festivals even young men don black boots, shirt and baggy pants, tucking a pistol into their belt to be fired into the air.

A remarkable feature of Cretan life is the ability of the islanders to maintain many aspects of their traditional culture in the face of a seasonal invasion of foreign tourists. Cretans have learned to coexist partly by operating in a different time-space continuum from their guests. From April to around October, the islanders live in the hurlyburly of the coastal resorts, running shops, pensions or tavernas. They then return to their traditional life in the hills for the autumn olive and grape harvest. Tourists eat early in the evening in restaurants along a harbour or beach while Cretans drive out to a village taverna for a dinner that begins around 11pm. Dance clubs play Western music until around 3am, when the Greek crowd arrives and the music switches to Cretan or Greek.

Men and women occupy different spheres. When not tending livestock or olive trees, Cretan men can usually be found in a *kafeneion* playing cards and drinking coffee or *raki*. Although exceptions are made for foreign women, *kafeneia* are off-limits to Cretan women who are usually occupied with housework and child rearing. In their spare time, women busy themselves with sewing, crocheting

The black-fringed kerchief and knee-high boots are classic pieces of traditional Cretan attire

or embroidery, often in a circle of other women. Old attitudes towards the 'proper role' for women are changing however, as more women enter the workforce. Friction has developed between the older generation and a younger generation more attuned to European norms.

The employment provided by tourism has enabled young people to remain on the island, thus allowing them to retain at least a nominal contact with their parents' culture.

Dos & Don'ts

If you go into a kafeneion, taverna or shop, greet the waiters or assistants with *kalimera* (good day) or *kalispera* (good evening). Personal questions are not considered rude, so prepare to be inundated with queries about your age, salary, marital status etc and to be showered with sympathy if you are over 25 and not married!

Cretans have a well-justified reputation for hospitality. The tradition was to treat strangers as honoured guests and invite them for coffee, a meal or to spend the night. Obviously Cretans are no longer offering free food and lodg-

Vendettas

Although Cretans share the same religious and ethnic background, homogeneity has not brought harmony. Cretans are notorious throughout Greece for murderous vendettas that have lasted for generations and caused hundreds of Cretans to flee the island. Particularly prevalent in Sfakia, the southwest of Crete, a vendetta can start over the theft of some sheep, an errant bullet at a wedding or anything deemed an insult to family honour. The insult is avenged with a murder, which must be avenged with another murder and so on. Modernity has in no way stemmed the carnage; in fact prosperity has allowed avengers to pursue their targets across Greece.

ing to several million tourists a year, but if you wander off the beaten track into mountain villages you may be invited to someone's home. If you're served a glass of water, coffee and some preserves it is the custom to first drink the water then eat the preserves and then drink the coffee. When visiting someone, it is bad manners to refuse the coffee or raki they'll offer you. You may feel uneasy, especially if your host is poor, but don't offend them by offering money. Give a gift instead, perhaps to a child in the family.

If you go out for a meal with Cretans, the bill is not shared but rather paid by the host. When drinking wine, only half fill the glass and don't let it become empty (a no-no).

Dolphin fresco replica, Knossos

Chris Christo

ARTS

Crete is rich in art treasures. The Minoan frescoes, with their fresh, bright colours, are extraordinarily naturalistic and have captured the imagination of experts and amateurs alike. Minoan pottery, called *Kamares* from the first finds in the Kamares cave, is also vivid and colourful and deals with nature themes. The art of fresco painting developed further in the 14th and 15th centuries when over 1000 churches were built and decorated with Byzantine-influenced frescoes. In the 16th and 17th centuries the Byzantine tradition was honed to perfection by the great icon painters Theophanes Sterlitzas and Mihail Damaskinos, who influenced the early work of El Greco.

The same period produced a rich body of literature. The era's masterpiece was undoubtedly the epic poem *Erotokritos* written by Vitzentzos Kornaros of Sitia in the late 16th or early 17th century. Cretan literature went into hibernation until the end of Turkish rule in the late 19th century. Ioannis Kondylakis (1861-1920) broke the ice with stories describing Greek village life, followed by the prolific Nikos Kazantzakis (p. 9), best known for *Zorba the Greek*.

El Greco

One of the geniuses of the Renaissance, El Greco (meaning 'The Greek' in Spanish) was born Domeniko Theotokopoulos in Iraklio (then called Candia) in 1541. In his early 20s he set out for Venice to further his studies in Titian's studio. But it was when he moved to Spain in 1577 that he really came into his own as a painter. His highly emotional style struck a chord with the Spanish, and the city of Toledo became home until his death in 1614. The only El Greco work on display in Crete is *View of Mt Sinai & the Monastery of St Catherine* (1570), painted during his time in Venice. It hangs in Iraklio's Historical Museum of Crete (p. 41).

highlights

Crete is famous as a sun-and-sea playground but if you can drag yourself from the white sand and luminous water you'll find museums, monasteries, archaeological sites, traditional villages and mythical caves. Fortunately, many of the top attractions are close together, allowing visitors to combine a beach, an archaeological site and a museum in a day trip.

History buffs will want to visit some of the **archaeological sites** from the Minoan and Roman eras. Knossos, the most famous site, is the only one where you're likely to feel crowded by other tourists. The relentless sun makes a hat and sunscreen essential.

Beaches are shadeless but you can rent a parasol and two lounge chairs for 1500 dr a day. There are also snack bars and showers on most beaches.

An integral part of the Cretan lifestyle is an afternoon siesta. From June to August, outside major cities, Cretans surrender to the afternoon heat and sack out from 1 to 5pm. If you arrive during these hours you will find the towns and villages eerily quiet, so it's best to get an early start.

Most museums and archaeological sites offer **discounts** but some are only available to EU residents. Students, teachers and pensioners from the EU often benefit from a 50% reduction. Students from outside the EU should invest in an ISIC (International Student Identity Card) as proof of student status.

Suggested Itineraries

Three Days Base yourself in Rethymno and visit the Old Quarter, fortress and museums. Spend 1 day in Hania's Old Quarter and another visiting the Archaeological Museum in Iraklio and the Minoan site of Knossos.

One Week Spend 2 days in Iraklio, then 3 in Hania, including a hike through the Samaria Gorge. Spend a day on the beach at Elafonisi, then 2 days in Rethymno. If you have time, take a day trip to Argiroupolis.

Two Weeks Spend 2 days in Iraklio and a night at a Lassithi Plateau village, visiting the Dikteon Cave and walking on the plateau. Head to Sitia, visit the archaeological museum, walk the gorge to Kato Zakros, visit ancient Zakros and have a swim. Have 2 days in Rethymno, with a day trip to Argiroupolis. Stay overnight in Agia Galini to visit Gortyn, Phaestos and Agia Triada. Spend 2 nights in the mountain town of Spili, or the resort of Plakias, and visit Moni Preveli and Preveli beach. Spend 2 nights in Hania, head down to Paleohora for 2 nights and spend a day hiking the Samaria Gorge. Unwind on Elafonisi beach the following day.

Chris Christo

The beautiful beaches of Cape Tigani, with the Gramvousa Islet beyond

ARCHAEOLOGICAL MUSEUM, IRAKLIO

(1, E9)

This outstanding museum is second in size and importance only to the National Archaeological Museum in Athens. You'll find, arranged in chronological order, pottery, jewellery, figurines and sarcophagi as well as the famous frescoes, mostly from Knossos and Agia Triada. All testify to the remarkable imagination and advanced skills of the Minoans. The exhibits are not well labelled but the glossy illustrated guide (2200 dr) by the museum's director will fill in the gaps for you.

The famous **Phaestos disc** (p. 29) is in Room 3. Inscribed on both sides of the 16cm disc are undeciphered symbols, whose meaning remains a mystery.

A striking exhibit, in Room 4, is the 20cm black stone **Bull's Head** from the Middle Minoan period, with fine curls, golden horns and amazingly lifelike eyes of painted crystal. Room 5 boasts some Linear A and B tablets – the Mycenaean Linear B script has been deciphered as household

Archaeological Receipts Fund

Middle Minoan black stone bull's head, with an impressive set of golden horns

Linear B

The deciphering of the Linear B script by English architect and part-time linguist Michael Ventris was the first tangible evidence that the Greek language had a recorded history longer than any scholar had previously believed. The mysterious scribblings turned out to be an archaic form of Greek 500 years older than the Ionic Greek used by Homer.

Linear B was written on clay tablets that laid undisturbed for centuries until unearthed at Knossos and later at several places on the Greek mainland. The tablets consisted of about 90 different signs dated from the 14th to the 13th century BC and were mainly inventories and records of commercial transactions, giving an indication of a fairly complex commercial structure.

or business accounts from the palace at Knossos.

The finds in Room 7 include the beautiful bee pendant found at Malia. Also in this room are the 3 celebrated vases from Agia Triada. Room 8 holds the finds from the palace at Zakros: don't miss the gorgeous little crystal vase that was found in over 300 pieces and was painstakingly put together again by museum staff.

The most famous and spectacular Minoan sarcophagus, the **sarcophagus from Agia Triada**, is upstairs in Room 14 (the Hall of Frescoes). This stone coffin is painted with floral and abstract designs and ritual scenes. Room 14 also hosts the most famous Minoan frescoes, including the amazing **Bull-Leaping Fresco** from Knossos, showing a seemingly double-jointed acrobat somersaulting on the back of a charging bull.

The famous, inscrutable Phaestos disc

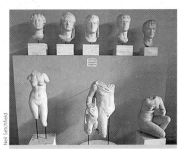

Five into three won't go

A stone damsel watches over a carved sarcophagus

DON'T MISS
- Kamares pottery • Phaestos disc • snake goddess figurine
- clay tablets with Linear A and Linear B scripts
- frescoes of Ladies in Blue, 'La Parisienne' and Dolphins

ARGIROUPOLIS   (2, E5)

When the summer heat becomes too intense even for the beach, you'll find a natural, outdoor air-conditioning system at Argiroupolis. The lower vil-

INFORMATION

- ✉ 25km southwest of Rethymno
- 🚌 Mon-Fri 2 buses daily from Rethymno (40mins, 460 dr)
- ✗ local tavernas

lage of this two-village town is a watery oasis formed by mountain springs that keep the temperature markedly cooler than the coast. Running through aqueducts, washing down walls, seeping from stones and pouring from spigots, the gushing spring water supplies the entire city of Rethymno. Towering chestnut and plane trees and luxuriant vegetation create a shady, restful spot, perfect for lingering over lunch in one of the local tavernas.

Argiroupolis is built on the remains of the ancient city of Lappa so there's plenty to explore. Founded by the Dorians, Lappa flourished under Roman rule when Emperor Augustus rewarded the city for its support in his war with Mark Antony. He built a reservoir in 27BC that is still in use today, and excavations have revealed a **Roman floor mosaic**, **Roman baths** and tombs. Archaeologists are continuing to excavate in the area and are turning up remnants of Lappa's history from its origins to its eventual destruction by the 9th-century Saracens.

Most of the houses in the upper village date from the last years of Turkish domination but you'll find odds and ends from Roman to Byzantine rule. The villagers maintain a traditional lifestyle but are proud of their heritage and eager to show you around.

Red-roofed houses afford a view of the Necropolis and the mountains beyond.

DON'T MISS
- waterfalls • Necropolis • 2000-year-old plane tree
- Agios Nikolaos church with 14th-century frescoes

ELAFONISI BEACH   (2, E2)

It's easy to understand why so many people rave about Elafonisi, at the southern extremity of Crete's west coast. The immense beach of shimmering white sand and blue waters creates a dreamy paradise. The main beach is flat and shadeless but you can rent umbrellas and beach chairs.

INFORMATION

- ✉ 80km southwest of Hania
- 🚌 daily buses from Hania (2½hrs, 1500 dr)
- ⚓ 2 boats a day from Paleohora in summer (1hr, 1140 dr)
- ✕ snack bars

An even better option is to head north across the sand. You'll soon cross about 50m of knee-deep water and come to the Elafonisi islet. The gently rolling dunes create a string of semi-secluded coves that often attract naturists. Waters are shallow along all the Elafonisi beaches making them great for young kids. Elafonisi is popular with day-trippers but there are two small hotels and a pension (on a bluff overlooking the main beach) for those who want to luxuriate in the quiet that descends here in the late afternoon.

White sand and shallow water make Elafonisi a favourite summer playground.

FRANGOKASTELLO (2, F5)

Frangokastello boasts the finest stretch of beach on the south coast as well as a crumbling fort, a small town, an eventful history and even ghosts. The wide, white-sand **beaches** are nearly deserted and slope gradually into shallow, warm water making them ideal for kids. Development has been kept to a minimum with most hotels set back from the shore to leave the natural beauty intact.

INFORMATION

- ✉ 82km southeast of Hania
- 🚌 in summer, 2 daily buses from Hora Sfakion to Plakias (1¼hrs, 1150 dr) via Frangokastello; from Hania a daily afternoon bus (2½hrs, 1750 dr); from Rethymno a daily bus (1¼hrs, 1550 dr)
- ✕ many restaurants and tavernas

Neil Setchfield

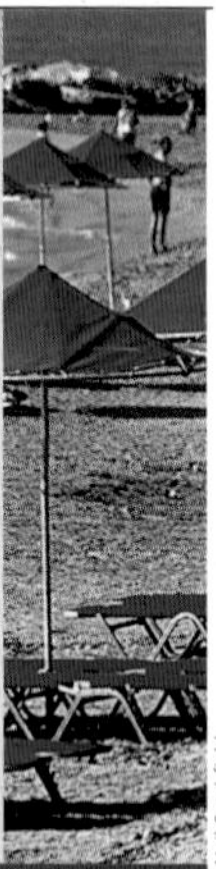

Neil Setchfield

The crumbling 14th-century fortress

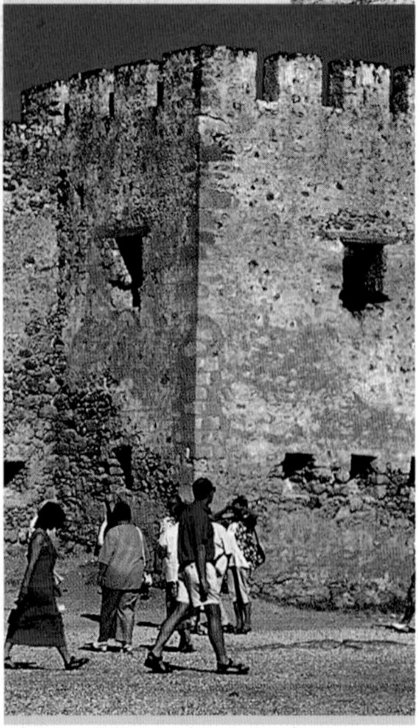

The best beach is beneath the 14th-century **fortress** built by the Venetians to protect the coast from pirates and help the Venetians deal with chronically rebellious Hora Sfakion 14km to the west. The Sfakia region continued to pose problems for the Turkish occupiers several centuries later. The legendary Sfakian patriot Ioannis Daskalogiannis led a disastrous rebellion against the Turks in 1770 and was persuaded to surrender himself to the Turks at the Frangokastello fortress. He was flayed alive. On May 17 1828, Hadzi Mihalis Dalanis led 385 rebels in a heroic last stand at the fortress. In one of the bloodiest battles of the Cretan struggle for independence, about 800 Turks were killed, along with Dalanis and the rebels.

The bloodshed gave rise to the legend of the *Drosoulites*. On the anniversary of the decisive battle or in late May around dawn, it's said that a procession of ghostly figures materialise around the fort and march to the sea. The phenomenon has been verified by a number of independent observers. Although locals believe the figures are the ghosts of slaughtered rebels, others theorise that it may be an optical illusion created by certain atmospheric conditions and that the figures may be a reflection of camels or soldiers in the Libyan Desert.

GORTYN   (2, F8)

The archaeological site of Gortyn (also called Gortina and Gortys) is the largest in Crete and one of the most fascinating. There's little here from the Minoan period because Gortyn was little more than a subject town of powerful Phaestos until it began accumulating riches (mostly from piracy) under the Dorians. By the 5th century BC, it was as influential as Knossos.

When Crete was under threat from the Romans the Gortynians cleverly made a pact with them and, when the Romans conquered the island in 67BC, they made Gortyn the island's capital. The city blossomed under Roman administrators who endowed it with lavish public buildings such as a **Praetorium**, amphitheatre, public bath, music school and temples. Except for the 7th century BC **Temple of the Pythian Apollo** and the 7th century AD Church of Agios Titos, most of what you see in Gortyn dates from the Roman period. Gortyn's centuries of splendour came to an end in 824 when the Saracens raided the island and destroyed the city.

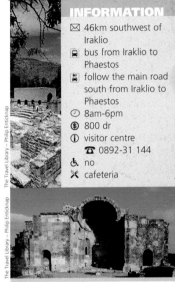

INFORMATION

✉ 46km southwest of Iraklio

🚌 bus from Iraklio to Phaestos

🚗 follow the main road south from Iraklio to Phaestos

🕐 8am-6pm

💲 800 dr

ℹ visitor centre

☎ 0892-31 144

♿ no

✗ cafeteria

The Roman-built Agios Titos Church

One can't help but be impressed by the size of the site and the sheer quantity of ruins but the most remarkable feature is the stone tablets engraved with the 6th century BC **Laws of Gortyn**. The Laws covered both civil and criminal matters. Criminal offences, no matter how serious, were usually punished by fines; there is no mention of imprisonment or execution.

Laws on inheritance, adoption and divorce were remarkably sensible. Division of property upon divorce closely resembled today's 'community property' legal theories. Wives retained the property they brought into the marriage, plus half of whatever they had 'woven within' the marriage. If the husband caused the divorce he had to pay a fine but, if he denied it, the case went before a judge. The departing wife was fined heavily if she carried off the husband's property but she had recourse in that situation as well. She could take an 'oath of denial' in front of the statue of Artemis, the archeress goddess, which would resolve the issue forever.

DON'T MISS   • Laws of Gortyn • plane tree (allegedly Zeus and Europa's love-nest) behind the Church of Agios Titos

KNOSSOS (2, E9)

Knossos, the capital of Minoan Crete, is the island's major attraction and one of the most significant archaeological finds of the century. Its ruins

INFORMATION

- ✉ 5km southeast of Iraklio
- ☎ 081-23 1940
- 🚌 bus No 2 leaves Iraklio's bus station A every 10 mins (20mins, 240 dr)
- 🕐 Apr-Oct: 8am-7pm; Nov-Mar: 8am-5pm
- 💲 1500 dr
- ✕ snack bar

were uncovered in 1900 by British archaeologist Sir Arthur Evans to the immense excitement of the archaeological world. Until he began his excavations no-one had suspected that a civilisation of this maturity and sophistication had existed in Europe at the time of the great Pharaohs of Egypt. Some even speculated that Knossos was the site of the lost city of Atlantis to which Plato referred many centuries later.

Unlike other archaeological sites in Crete, substantial reconstruction helps you visualise what the Palace might have looked like at the peak of its glory. Evans maintained that he was obliged to rebuild columns and supports in reinforced concrete or the Palace would have collapsed, but many archaeologists feel that the integrity of the site was irretrievably damaged.

Because Evans financed the entire endeavour from his own pocket however, he had the freedom to turn his own vision of Minoan architecture into a reality that even the uninitiated can appreciate. On your wanders you will come across many of Evans' reconstructed columns; most are painted deep brown-red with gold-trimmed black capitals. These, like all Minoan columns, taper at the bottom.

A remnant of the palace wall features a coloured bull relief and tapering columns.

The first palace at Knossos was built around 1900BC but most of what you see dates from 1700BC after the Old Palace was destroyed by an earthquake. The New Palace was carefully designed to meet the needs of a complex society. There were domestic quarters for the king or queen, residences for officials and priests, homes of common folk and burial grounds. Public reception rooms, shrines, workshops, treasuries and storerooms were built around a paved courtyard in a design so intricate that it may have been behind the legend of the Labyrinth and the Minotaur.

Strategically placed copies of **Minoan frescoes** help infuse the site with the artistic spirit of these remarkable people, but the Minoan achievements in plumbing equal their achievements in painting. Drains and pipes were carefully placed to avoid flooding, taking advantage of centrifugal force. It appears that at some points water ran uphill, demonstrating a mastery of the principle that water finds its own level. The Queen's bathroom even had a toilet that flushed (water was poured down by hand).

Explore the restored ruins

Other highlights include the famous **throne room** – just look for the queue. Although the room itself is fenced off, you can get a good view from an outer room. The room is thought to have been a shrine, and the throne the seat of a high priestess, rather than a king. It has an aura of mysticism and reverence rather than pomp and ceremony. The Minoans did not worship their goddesses in great temples but in small shrines (each palace had several). The centrepiece – the simple, beautifully proportioned throne – is flanked by the **Griffin Fresco**. Griffins were mythical beasts, sacred to the Minoans.

Next to the throne room and on the 1st floor is the section Evans called the **Piano Nobile**, where he believed the reception and state rooms were. A room at the northern end of this floor displays copies of some of the frescoes found at Knossos.

Returning to the Central Court, the impressive grand staircase leads from the middle of the eastern side of the palace to the **royal apartments**, which Evans called the Domestic Quarter. Most of the apartments are closed to the public but you can still see a copy of the exquisite **Dolphin Fresco** that may have graced the wall or floor of the Queen's megaron (central hall).

DON'T MISS
- throne room • Piano Nobile • royal apartments
- Pithoi (giant storage urns) • Hall of the Double Axes

LASSITHI PLATEAU   (2, E11)

The first view of the mountain-fringed Lassithi Plateau, laid out like an immense patchwork quilt, is stunning. The plateau, 900m above sea level, is a vast expanse of pear and apple orchards, almond trees and fields of crops, dotted by some 7000 windmills. These are not conventional stone windmills, but slender metal constructions with white canvas sails built under Venetian rule to irrigate the land. Unfortunately the original windmills are rarely used today but you may see a few examples outside tavernas or shops. There are 20 villages dotted around the periphery of the plateau, the largest of which is Tzermiado, with 1300 inhabitants, a bank, post office and OTE (telephone centre).

The plateau's rich soil has been cultivated since Minoan times. The inaccessibility of the region made it a hotbed of insurrection during Venetian and Turkish rule. Following an uprising in the 13th century, the Venetians drove out the inhabitants of Lassithi and destroyed their orchards. The plateau lay abandoned for 200 years.

Lassithi's major sight is the **Dikteon Cave**, just outside the village of Psyhro. Here, according to mythology, Rhea hid the newborn Zeus from Cronos, his offspring-gobbling father. The cave,

Locals share conversation and food at an outdoor cafe.

Neil Setchfield

An abandoned windmill stands motionless among wildflowers.

which has both stalactites and stalagmites, was excavated in 1900 by British archaeologist David Hogarth. He found numerous votives indicating that the cave was a place of cult worship. These finds are housed in the Archaeological Museum in Iraklio. A guide is not essential for a tour of the cave, but a torch and sensible shoes are. The path to the cave is pretty rough, and the cave itself is slippery.

See page 62 for a walking tour through the plateau, from Tzermiado to Psyhro.

The Lassithi Plateau's rich soil has been cultivated for millennia.

HANIA'S OLD QUARTER (5)

Hania is Crete's most evocative city, with a wealth of buildings from its former Venetian and Turkish overlords scattered throughout its narrow, stone streets. Don't be discouraged by the carapace of modern development that presses around the Old Town. Remnants of Venetian walls still border a web of atmospheric streets that tumble onto a magnificent harbour. The Venetian townhouses along the harbourside promenade (5, E3) have been restored and converted into pensions, restaurants, cafes and shops.

The massive **fortifications** built by the Venetians are still impressive. The best-preserved section is the western wall (5, E2), running from the fortress to the Promahonas hill. It was built in 1538 as part of a defensive system when the Turks were looking to expand their real-estate holdings in the Mediterranean. The engineer, Michele Sanmichele, also designed Iraklio's defences. The **lighthouse** (5, D3) at the entrance to the harbour is the most visible of the Venetian monuments. It looks in need of tender loving care these days, but makes a fine silhouette against the sky, especially at sunset.

Hania's war-torn history has left it with only a few impressive monuments but the city wears its scars proudly. Walk along Zambeliou (5, F4), Theotokopoulou (5, E3) and Angelou (5, E3) streets in the Old Quarter and you'll come across roofless Venetian buildings turned into gracious outdoor restaurants. Many of the timber houses that date from Turkish rule have been restored.

Even during the height of the tourist season when the buildings are festooned with technicolour beach towels and similar claptrap, Hania retains the exoticism of a city caught between east and west.

INFORMATION

✉ south of the harbour to Giannari
ⓘ tourist office
(☎ 0821-92 943; fax 0821-92 624), Kriari 40, close to Plateia 1866
♿ no
✖ see page 79-80

Hania's atmospheric Old Town

John Elk III

Neil Setchfield

DON'T MISS

- Venetian wall • Mosque of the Janissaries (p. 36-7)
- harbour promenade • Zambeliou St

MONI PREVELI & PREVELI BEACH   (2, F6)

The well-maintained Moni Preveli stands in splendid isolation high above the Libyan Sea. From the parking lot outside the monastery, there's a lookout with a panoramic view over the southern coast. The view alone is worth the trip, but the monastery itself has an interesting history.

The origins of the monastery are unclear because most historical documents were lost in the many attacks inflicted upon it over the centuries. The year 1701 is carved on the monastery fountain but it may have been founded much earlier. Like most of Crete's monasteries, it played a significant role in the rebellion against Turkish rule. It became a centre of resistance during 1866, causing the Turks to set fire to it and destroy its crops. After the WWII Battle of Crete, many Allied soldiers were sheltered here by Abbot Agathangelos before their evacuation to Egypt. In retaliation, the Germans plundered the monastery. The monastery's **museum** contains a candelabra presented by grateful British soldiers after the war.

Built in 1835, the church is worth a visit for the wonderful **icon screen** containing a gaily painted *Adam & Eve in Paradise* by the monk Mihail Prevelis.

The monks' quarters

INFORMATION	
✉	37km south of Rethymno
🚌	2 daily buses in summer from Rethymno to Moni Preveli (1hr, 1200 dr)
⛴	daily boat from Plakias to Preveli beach
🕐	Mar-May: 8am-7pm; June-Oct: 8am-1.30pm & 3.30-8pm
💲	700 dr (monastery)
✖	snack bars on the beach

From the road to the monastery, a track leads downhill to **Preveli beach**, one of Crete's most photographed beaches. This idyllic spot, at the mouth of the Kourtaliotis gorge, is fringed with oleander bushes and palm trees. The River Megalopotamos cuts the beach in half on its way into the Libyan Sea. Walk up the palm-lined banks of the river and you'll come to cold, freshwater pools ideal for swimming.

Cover Up

Like most monasteries, Moni Preveli requires women to cover their legs. If you arrive in shorts, you can borrow a skirt at the entrance. The skirts are ugly enough to ensure you won't be tempted to walk away with one.

MONI TOPLOU (2, D14)

The imposing Moni Toplou looks more like a fortress than a monastery, a necessity given the dangers it faced at the time of its construction.

The middle of the 15th century was marked by piracy, banditry and constant rebellions. The monks defended themselves with all the means at their disposal including a heavy gate, cannons (the name Toplou is Turkish for 'with a cannon'), and small holes for pouring boiling oil onto the heads

of their attackers. Nevertheless, the monastery was sacked by pirates in 1498, looted by the Knights of Malta in 1530, looted by the Turks in 1646 and captured by the Turks in 1821.

With the wealth and treasure that the monastery had accumulated, it's not surprising that it was a tempting target for looters. The star attraction is undoubtedly the **icon** *Lord Thou Art Great* by Koannis Kornaros. Each of the 61 small scenes is beautifully worked and each is inspired by a phrase from the Orthodox prayer that begins 'Lord, Thou Art Great'. The icon is in the church, along with 14th-century frescoes in the north aisle and an antique icon stand from 1770.

Toplou monastery's activism in the cause for Cretan independence came at a heavy price. Under the Turkish occupation, its reputation for hiding rebels led to severe reprisals. During WWII it sheltered many resistance leaders and operated an underground radio transmitter that led to the execution of Abbot Silignakis.

Moni Toplou has endured sacking and looting over the centuries.

DON'T MISS
• Kornaros icon featuring 61 scenes • 2nd century BC engraving of the Treaty of Magnesia

PHAESTOS   (2, F8)

Phaestos was second only to Knossos as the most important palace city of Minoan Crete. Of all the Minoan sites, Phaestos has the most awe-inspiring location, with all-encompassing views of the **Messara plain** and **Mt Ida**. The best time to visit is in spring when the flowers are in bloom.

Phaestos Disc

Where did it come from and what was it used for? Archaeologists have debated the significance of the Phaestos disc ever since its discovery in 1903. Both faces of the 16cm clay disc are inscribed with mysterious hieroglyphics arranged in a spiral pattern. The disc dates from around 1700BC, and Sir Evans believed it may have been brought from Asia. Other scholars believe that it was a local product, possibly with a sacred purpose. The enigmatic disc is now in Iraklio's Archaeological Museum (p. 16-17).

INFORMATION

✉ 61km southwest of Iraklio

🚌 8 daily buses (5 in winter) from Iraklio's bus station B (2hrs, 1250 dr)

🕐 8am-7pm

💲 1200 dr

ℹ visitor centre
☎ 0892-42 315

♿ no

✕ on-site cafeteria

The layout of the palace is identical to Knossos, with rooms arranged around a central court, but Sir Arthur Evans didn't get his hands on Phaestos so there has been no reconstruction. Also in contrast to Knossos, Phaestos has yielded very few frescoes; it seems the palace walls were mostly covered with a layer of white gypsum. There was an old palace here that was destroyed at the end of the Middle Minoan period. Parts of it have been excavated and its ruins are partially superimposed upon the new palace.

Step aerobics for the Minoans

The entrance to the new palace is by the 15m-wide **Grand Staircase** which leads to the western side of the **Central Court**. The best-preserved parts of the palace complex are the **reception rooms** and **private apartments** to the north of the Central Court; excavations continue here. This section was entered via an imposing portal with half-columns at either side, the lower parts of which are still *in situ*. Unlike the Minoan freestanding columns, these do not taper at the base. The celebrated Phaestos disc was found in a building to the north of the palace.

RETHYMNO'S OLD QUARTER (4)

Rethymno's old Venetian-Ottoman quarter is a maze of narrow streets, graceful wood-balconied houses and ornate Venetian monuments, with minarets adding a touch of the Orient. Architectural similarities invite comparison with Hania, but Rethymno has a character of its own and boasts of being the most culturally aware city on Crete. The area occupies the headland north of Dimakopoulou, which runs from Plateia Vardinogianni on the west coast to Plateia Iroön in the east (becoming Gerakari en route).

INFORMATION

- ✉ north of Dimakopoulou
- ☉ 8am-8pm (fortress)
- ⑤ 800 dr (fortress)
- ⓘ municipal tourist office ☎ 0831-29 148
- ♿ no
- ✗ see page 84-5

Neil Setchfield

Character in the Old Quarter

Neil Setchfield

A 16th-century **fortress** (4, E2) stands on Paleokastro hill, the site of the city's ancient acropolis. Many buildings once stood within its massive walls but now only a church and a mosque survive intact. The ramparts offer good views, while the site has lots of ruins to explore.

Pride of place among the many vestiges of Venetian rule (1210-1645) goes to the **Rimondi Fountain** (4, F5) with its spouting lion heads, and the 16th-century **loggia**. (4, F6). At the southern end of Ethnikis Antistaseos is the well-preserved **Porto Guora** (Great Gate; 4, H5), a remnant of the Venetian defensive wall.

The old quarter's twisting streets make it easy to get lost in. Coming from the south, the best way to approach is through the Porto Guora onto Ethnikis Antistaseos. This busy shopping street leads to the Rimondi Fountain. The area around here is thick with cafes, restaurants and souvenir shops.

DON'T MISS
- Venetian fortress • Rimondi Fountain • Nerandzes Mosque
- Venetian loggia

SAMARIA GORGE   (2, E3)

A visit to this stupendous gorge is an experience to remember. You'll descend the gorge, enveloped in the scent of pine, until you reach the riverbed. Along the way you might see owls, eagles or vultures. If you're extremely lucky you might spot the lammergeier (bearded vulture), harrier eagle or golden eagle, all endangered species. The gorge's

Feet First

It's essential to have the right footwear as you will be picking your way over pointed rocks for much of the trek. Trainers will do but hiking boots with ankle support are best. When the going gets tough, just think of the glorious swim on Agia Roumeli beach that awaits at the end of the hike.

inaccessibility saved it from the twin evils of timber cutting and livestock grazing. As a result, the gorge is teeming with life. There's an incredible number of wildflowers, at their best in April and May. Watch for rare peonies that flourish in the dampness of the gorge.

The gorge is home to the *zouridha* (Cretan polecat) and the *kri-kri*, a wild goat that survives in the wild only here and on the islet of Kri-Kri. The gorge was made a national park in 1962 to save the kri-kri from extinction but you're unlikely to see one of these timid creatures.

At 18km, Samaria is supposedly the longest gorge in Europe, beginning just below the Omalos plateau, carved out by the river that flows between the Lefka Ori and Mt Volakias. The best way to see the gorge is on a trek (p. 61) but you won't be alone. Samaria attracts several thousand visitors a day in July and August making it uncomfortably crowded at times. You should bring something to eat but there's no need to take water. While it's inadvisable to drink from the main stream, there are plenty of springs along the way spurting delicious cool water straight from the rock. Swimming or spending the night in the gorge is forbidden.

INFORMATION

- ✉ 44km south of Hania
- 🚌 4 buses daily from Hania to Xyloskalo (1hr, 1250 dr)
- 🕐 Apr-Oct: 6am-4pm
- 💲 1200 dr
- ℹ ☎ 0821-67 179
- ✗ none – bring your own

John Elk III

Neil Setchfield

If the climb doesn't take your breath away, the scenery will.

SITIA (2, E14)

Sitia is the perfect escape from the tourist frenzy that can grip most of the north coast in summer. You will not see shop after shop of cookie-cutter ceramics; waiters will not try to drag you into their restaurants; menus are not translated into four languages. What you will see are ordinary Cretans going about their business in an attractive, mid-sized coastal town.

INFORMATION

- ✉ 73km east of Agios Nikolaos
- 🚌 5 buses daily from Agios Nikolaos (1½hrs, 1500 dr)
- ⓘ Sultana Festival in mid-August
- ✕ see page 87

The **harbourside promenade** is clear of taverna tables, making it a lovely venue for an early evening stroll. The bustling streets of the **old town** wind their way uphill from the harbour while the town's southern end is on a long, narrow stretch of sandy beach. Even at the height of the season, the town has a laid-back feel that is a refreshing antidote to the commercialism of Agios Nikolaos.

Excavations indicate that a fairly substantial settlement existed here in Minoan times but evidence of a town in the classical and Roman periods remains sketchy. Sitia was the seat of a bishopric in the Byzantine era and gained renewed prestige as Venice's major stronghold in the east.

The walled town was twice damaged by earthquakes under the Venetians and subject to relentless raids by the Turkish pirate Barbarossa, culminating in a devastating attack in 1538. A little over a century later the Turks swept into town, sacking the city and forcing the residents out. It wasn't until 1870 that Sitia was repopulated by the Turks, who made it an administrative centre. Sitia was the birthplace of Vinzetzos Kornaros, author of the 16th-century epic *Erotokritos*.

Sitia's very strollable harbourside promenade

DON'T MISS
- Folklore Museum • Archaeological Museum • Venetian fort
- Roman fish tanks • harbourside promenade

ZAKROS PALACE & KATO ZAKROS (2, E15)

A visit to Zakros Palace and Kato Zakros combines two of the best things about Crete: an intriguing archaeological site and a long stretch of under-populated beach.

Although **Zakros Palace** was the last Minoan palace to have been discovered, the excavations proved remarkably fruitful. The exquisite rock-crystal vase and stone Bull's Head now in Iraklio's Archaeological Museum (p. 16-17) were found at Zakros Palace, along with a treasure-trove of Minoan antiquities. **Ancient Zakros**, the smallest of Crete's four palace complexes, was a major port in Minoan times, trading with Egypt, Syria, Anatolia and Cyprus. The palace consisted of royal apartments, storerooms and workshops flanking a central courtyard.

The Travel Library – Peter Terry

INFORMATION

✉ 118km southeast of Agios Nikolaos, 45km southeast of Sitia

🚌 2 buses daily to Zakros (via Paleokastro) from Sitia (1hr, 1000 dr); in summer the buses continue to Kato Zakros

🕐 Tues-Sun 8.30am-3pm (ancient Zakros)

💲 500 dr (ancient Zakros)

✗ tavernas in Kato Zakros

The town occupied a low plain close to the shore. Water levels have risen over the years so that some parts of the palace complex are submerged. The ruins are not well preserved, but a visit to the site is worthwhile for its wild and remote setting. The village of Zakros, 7km away, is the nearest permanent settlement to the coastal Minoan site of Zakros.

Kato Zakros, next to the site, is a beautiful little seaside settlement that springs to life between March and October. If the weather is dry, there is a lovely 2hr walk from Zakros to Kato Zakros through a gorge known as the Valley of the Dead because of the cave tombs dotted along the cliffs. The trail emerges close to the Minoan site.

The tiny village of **Xerokambos**, on the next bay south of Kato Zakros, is an unspoilt haven near several coves of inviting pale sand.

The Travel Library – Peter Terry

Once a bustling Minoan Port, Zakros' appeal is now its wild coastal setting.

CRETE LOWLIGHTS

Ever since the national road along the north coast opened in 1972, the coast between Iraklio and Malia has seen a frenzy of development. A concrete wall of hotels, schnitzel outlets and tacky souvenir shops lines every stretch of sandy beach along here. Although none of the resorts along this stretch would win any beauty contests, **Hersonisos** (2, D11) and **Malia** (2, E11) set a new standard in dreariness. For many Cretans, they typify everything that's wrong with mass tourism.

In both resorts, the local population has retreated to pleasant little hill villages behind the main road and left the lower beachfront towns to wallow in crass commercialism. From the frozen fish in the seaside restaurants to the imported 'Cretan' ceramics in the souvenir shops, nothing is authentic. The music in bars and tavernas is either western or the most westernised Greek music available. If you don't understand Greek letters, don't worry – you won't see a single one in Hersonisos and Malia. Fish & chips stands, cafes with names like 'Cheers' and 'Union Jack', and video bars playing British sitcoms seem designed to shield visitors from the horrible realisation that they are actually in a foreign country.

Hersonisos v Malia

Although Hersonisos and Malia are often considered identical examples of atrocious overdevelopment, there are subtle differences. Both places chase bargain-hunting package tourists but Hersonisos has a few luxury hotels on the outskirts. The crowds are young in both towns but in Malia you'll feel decrepit if you're over 22. In Hersonisos you drink to get drunk, dance and wake up with a stranger while at Malia you drink to get drunk, fall down and wake up on the pavement. If that sounds good, you know where to go.

Wall-to-wall concrete in the resort town of Hersonisos

Neil Setchfield

sights & activities

AGIOS NIKOLAOS (3)

Agios Nikolaos, or 'Ag Nik' as it's familiarly known, emerged as a port for the city-state of Lato (p. 46) in the early Hellenistic years but never amounted to much until mass tourism came along. The Venetians had a harbour slightly northwest of today's town but there's no trace of the Venetian occupation except for the name they gave to the surrounding gulf: Mirabello, or 'beautiful view'.

The town was resettled in the mid-19th century by fleeing rebels from Sfakia and it was later named capital of the Lassithi region. In the early 1960s, it became a chic hideaway for the likes of Jules Dassin and Walt Disney and by the end of the decade package tourists were arriving in force.

The beaches outside town are mediocre but the heart of the town is an irresistibly fetching conjunction of lake and harbour. Even though the waterside has been shamelessly overbuilt with bars, shops and restaurants, the natural beauty of the setting hasn't been entirely extinguished.

Aquarium of Agios Nikolaos (3, D1)

This museum has interesting displays of fish as well as information about diving (including PADI courses) and snorkelling throughout Crete.

✉ Akti Koundourou
☎ 0841-24 953
🕐 Apr-Oct: Mon-Sat 10am-9pm; Nov-Mar: 10am-4pm 💲 1300/800 dr (children under 12)

Archaeological Museum (3, E1)

This modern building houses a large, well-displayed collection from eastern Crete. The exhibits, which span the Neolithic period to the early 1st century, are especially noted for findings from early Minoan graves. Don't miss the highly stylised Goddess of Myrtos libation vase.

✉ Paleologou 74 ☎ 0841-22 462 🕐 Tues-Sun 8.30am-3pm
💲 500 dr

Folk Museum (3, G3)

This museum displays an interesting collection of fine embroidery, woven rugs, antique clothing, utensils, armaments and musical instruments.

✉ Paleologou 2 🕐 Sun-Fri 10am-3pm 💲 250 dr

Voulismeni Lake (3, G2)

It's been given names ranging from Xepatomeni ('bottomless') to Voulismeni ('sunken') to Vromolimni ('dirty'), but it's not bottomless (at 64m) nor is it dirty any more. The area around this picturesque lake, ringed with tavernas and cafes, is the most interesting in town.

✉ 200m north of Plateia Venizelou

Lake and harbour converge to form Agios Nikolaos' lively waterfront.

Neil Setchfield

HANIA (5)

Hania is famous for its wonderful old Venetian quarter (p. 26), but there's lots more to discover in Crete's second city and former capital. Hania has a lively tradition of artisanship, making it a great shopping city, and the inner harbour is ideal for relaxing in a cafe and watching the passing promenade. The covered food market, modelled after the one in Marseilles, presents a colourful panoply of Cretan products. To escape the crowds, take a stroll around the **Splantzia quarter** (5, E7), a delightful tangle of narrow streets and little plateias, or head out to the beach. **Nea Hora** (5, E1) is the town beach, just west of the fortress, but the water is not particularly clean. For better swimming, keep heading west to Oasis Beach, which ends at Kalamaki beach after about 5km.

Archaeological Museum (5, F4)

Housed in the 16th-century Venetian Church of San Francisco, this museum displays great finds from western Crete dating from the Neolithic to the Roman era, including statues, pottery, coins, jewellery, three splendid floor mosaics and some impressive painted sarcophagi. The Turkish fountain in the grounds is a relic from the building's days as a mosque.
✉ **Halidon 21** ☎ 0821-53 033 ⏰ Tues-Sun 8.30am-5pm
💲 500 dr

Covered Market (5, G6)

Whether or not you are self-catering you should at least feast your eyes on this magnificent covered food market; it makes all other food markets look like stalls at a church bazaar. Unfortunately, the central bastion of the city wall was demolished to make way for this fine cruciform creation, built in 1911.
✉ **Plateia Hortatson** ⏰ Mon-Sat 7am-2pm; also Tues, Thurs & Fri 5-8.30pm

Mosque of the Janissaries (5, E4)

Given what the Cretans suffered from the Janissaries, it's surprising that this 17th-century mosque wasn't torn apart when Turkish rule ended. Instead, it was carefully restored and is the most eye-catching monu-

Feast your eyes at the Covered Market

Neil Setchfield

Neil Setchfield

Hania's Naval Museum is worth a stop.

ment on the Venetian waterfront. It's used today as an exhibition space.

✉ **Akti Tobazi**

Naval Museum (5, D3)
In the fortress overlooking the Venetian port you'll find an interesting collection of model ships, naval instruments, paintings and photographs.

✉ **inner harbour**
☎ **0821-91 875** 🕐
Tues-Sun 10am-2pm
💲 **400 dr**

Site of Ancient Kidonia (5, E5)
Hania sits on top of the ancient city of Kidonia which was allegedly founded by Kidon, grandson of King Minos. The remains here may have been the site of a palace destroyed in the fire of 1450BC. Kidonia became an important site under the Dorians and then the Romans, Byzantines and Venetians. Each group built over the remains of the prior occupation, which means that a full excavation of ancient Kidonia would require tearing up most of modern Hania.

✉ **junction of Kanevaro and Kandanoleu**

The Janissaries

Under the Ottoman system, the Sultan pressed Christian boys from subject populations into service. They were converted to Islam, given special training and made part of the Ottoman army elite. Known as Janissaries, they functioned as the Sultan's administrative representatives throughout the Ottoman Empire. Although they were forbidden to marry, they were granted special privileges. On Crete, the rule of the Janissaries spun out of control. Christian families on Crete who had initially thought the Ottoman Janissary system an honour for their sons were horrified to discover that the Janissaries on their island were more like hoodlums. They answered to no law but their own and ruthlessly terrorised the population with extortionate taxes, random attacks and even murder. When the Janissaries staged a widespread revolt in 1826, the Sultan finally ended the system.

Neil Setchfield

You can't miss Hania's Mosque of the Janissaries.

IERAPETRA (2, F12)

Ierapetra is Crete's most southerly major town. It was an important city for the Dorians and the last city to fall to the Romans, who made it a major port of call in their conquest of Egypt. Despite its antiquity virtually nothing survives from the classical period. The city languished under the Venetians, although there is a small Venetian-built fortress at the western end of the harbour. In recent years agriculture has made the town wealthy enough to finance the restoration of the old town and the harbourside. Although the city has a long, narrow strip of grey-sand beach it attracts few tourists. After the tourist hype of Agios Nikolaos, the unpretentiousness of Ierapetra is refreshing.

Archaeological Museum

This small museum displays a collection of headless classical statuary and a superb statue of the goddess Demeter that dates from the 2nd century AD. Also notable is a *larnax*, or clay coffin, dating from around 1300BC. The chest is decorated with 12 painted panels showing hunting scenes, an octopus and a chariot procession among other scenes.

✉ Adrianou 1 ☎ 0842-622 246 ⏱ Tues-Sun 8.30am-3pm ⑤ free

Old Town

Just inland from the harbour, the labyrinthine streets of the old town provide a delightful glimpse of small-town life. You'll see matrons in black watching kids kicking soccer balls while the laundry dries on clotheslines over the streets.

✉ inland from the south harbour near the Venetian fortress

Venetian Fortress

Built in the early years of Venetian rule and strengthened by Francesco Morosini in 1626, the fortress has recently been restored. You can visit it but there's not much to see.

✉ **western harbour** ⏱ **Tues-Sun 8.30am-3pm** ⑤ **free**

Refreshingly untouristy – Ierapetra's grey-sand beach

Neil Setchfield

IMBROS GORGE   (2, E5)

The Imbros Gorge, though less visited than its illustrious sister at Samaria, is just as beautiful. Cypresses, holm-oaks, fig and almond trees gradually thin to just cypress and Jerusalem sage deep within the gorge. The narrowest width of the ravine is 2m while the walls of rock reach 300m in height. At only 8km the Imbros walk is also much easier on the feet.

You can begin in the south at the village of **Komitades** (2, F5) but most people begin in the little mountain village of **Imbros** (2, E5). Both places have plenty of minimarkets and tavernas to fuel up. If you start from Imbros you'll find the well-marked entrance to the gorge next to a taverna, just outside Imbros village on the road to Hora Sfakion. The track is easy to follow as it traces the stream-bed past rockslides and caves. The gorge path ends at the village of Komitades, from where you can either walk or take a taxi to Hora Sfakion (2, F5), 5km away.

The Imbros Gorge is 57km southeast of Hania. Contact Hania's tourist office (☎ 0821-92 943; fax 0821-92 624) for information. Three buses daily from Hania to Hora Sfakion stop at Imbros village (1½hrs, 1100 dr).

Rebel Stronghold

Like most gorges in Sfakia, the Imbros sheltered Sfakian rebels during the Turkish occupation. The Sfakians knew how to take full advantage of their mountainous terrain and this made them effective fighters against the Turks. In 1941, 12,000 Allied survivors of the Battle of Crete were led to the southern coast through the Imbros Gorge and were under attack most of the way.

The rugged beauty of Imbros Gorge

IRAKLIO (1)

Hectic, noisy and traffic-ridden, Iraklio is mainly viewed as a grim necessity to be endured for the sake of archaeology. After the obligatory Archaeological Museum-Knossos visit, most visitors hurry away to more inviting spots. Yet, as Crete's capital and Greece's fifth-largest city, Iraklio manages to achieve a certain urban sophistication despite its poor infrastructure. The city is prosperous; many neighbourhoods have been rebuilt and there are enough drachmas around to support a thriving cafe scene and lively nightlife.

The Archaeological Museum (p. 16) and the palace of Knossos (p. 22) are a window into Minoan culture but Iraklio abounds in other reminders of a turbulent history. The 14th-century Venetian walls and fortress underscore the importance of Iraklio (then called Candia) to the Venetians. Many monuments date from Venetian occupation. Notice the Morosini fountain (1, E6), the Venetian loggia (1, D6) and the Agios Markos church (1, E6), opposite Plateia Venizelou on 25 Avgoustou.

The Turks finally penetrated the fortified city in 1669 after a 22-year siege – the longest in European history – and made Iraklio their commercial centre. On 25 August 1898 a Turkish mob massacred hundreds of Cretans, 17 British soldiers and the British Consul in Iraklio. Within weeks, a squadron of British ships steamed into Iraklio's harbour and forever ended Turkish rule on Crete.

Battle of Crete Museum (1, E9)
This absorbing museum chronicles the historic Battle of Crete (May 1941) through photographs, letters, uniforms and weapons. ✉ **corner of Doukos Dofor and Hatzidaki** ☎ **081-346 554** ⊘ **9am-1pm** ⑤ **free**

Bembo Fountain
(1, G6) The fountain was built by the Venetians in the 16th century from a hotchpotch of building materials including an ancient statue. The ornate edifice next to the fountain was added by the Turks. ✉ **southern end of 1866 St**

Church of Agia Ekaterini of Sinai
(1, F4) This 16th-century church was a dependency of the church of the same name on Mt Sinai. It is now a museum boasting a superb collection of icons from the 'Cretan Renaissance' including the 6 painted by El Greco's mentor, Mihail Damaskinos. ✉ **Plateia Ekaterini** ☎ **081-24 2111** ⊘ **Mon-Sat 9am-1.30pm; also Tues, Thurs & Fri 5-8pm** ⑤ **500 dr**

City Walls (1, J6)
Iraklio burst out of these walls long ago but the

A Bunch of Bull?

After King Minos' wife, Pasiphae, gave birth to the Minotaur, they say that her lover, the bull, went wild and laid waste to the Cretan countryside, tearing up crops and stamping down orchard walls. Something had to be done.

Help arrived in the form of iron-man Heracles. The man who once killed a lion with his bare hands came to Crete to kill the bull. It was the 7th of his 12 mighty feats. The monstrous animal was belching flames and fumes but Heracles captured it single-handedly and took it away. The ancient Cretans were so grateful that they named Minos' port city after their superman. That is how Iraklio (Iraklion, Heraklion) got its name.

massive fortifications, with 7 bastions and 4 gates, are still conspicuous. You can follow the walls around the heart of the city for a view of Iraklio's neighbourhoods, but it is not particularly scenic.

Historical Museum of Crete (1, C5)
Fascinating items include the only El Greco painting you'll see in Crete, a reconstruction of Kazantzakis' library, and dramatic photos of Iraklio during the Battle of Crete.
✉ cnr **Venizelou & Grevenon** ☎ 081-28 3219 ⏱ summer: Mon-Fri 9am-5pm, Sat 9am-2pm; winter: Mon-Sat 9.30am-2.30pm ⑤ 1000 dr

Morosini Fountain
(1, E6) Four lions spurt water into 8 ornate, U-shaped marble troughs in this most famous Venetian fountain. The fountain is not named after the sculptor but after Francesco Morosini, the Venetian

The Venetian-built Bembo Fountain

politician who commissioned it in 1628.
✉ **Plateia Venizelou**

Rocca al Mare Fortress (1, A8)
The 16th-century Venetian fortress stopped the Turks for 22 years and then became a Turkish prison for Cretan rebels. The exterior is most impressive, with reliefs of the Lion of St Mark. The interior has 26 overly-restored rooms and good views from the top.

✉ **Old Harbour jetty** ☎ 081-24 6211 ⏱ Mon-Sat 8am-6pm, Sun 10am-3pm ⑤ 500 dr

Tomb of Nikos Kazantzakis (1, J6)
Always in trouble with the church for his oft-expressed skepticism, Kazantzakis was given a burial service at Agios Minos Cathedral, but the church refused to grant him a religious burial.
✉ **Martinengo Bastion in the southern part of town**

The imposing Rocca al Mare Fortress withstood a 22-year Turkish siege.

KRITSA (2, E12)

Kritsa village is a charmer from every angle. As you approach from below, the swathe of whitewashed houses terraced into the mountainside is striking. From the 600m-high village, there are sweeping views over the valley on one side and steep mountains on the other. The village is a carnival of colour, with Kritsa's renowned weavings and embroidery draped and hung on every available surface. Even the busloads of tourists who swarm through the streets all summer haven't managed to dim Kritsa's allure. If you're visiting in late August, don't miss the traditional 'wedding' staged by the villagers.

As in many Cretan villages, the men are in *kafeneia* while the women run the shops. When not hawking their merchandise, the women sit on stools with fingers flying over their fabric. Although the designs have been bastardised to fit tourist tastes, try to search out the traditional geometric designs of Crete.

Kritsa is also within easy reach of two other sights: the **Church of Panagia Kera** (p. 48) and the archaeological site of **Lato** (p. 46).

Kritsa is 11km southwest of Agios Nikolaos. The tourist office of Agios Nikolaos (☎ 0841-22 357; fax 0841-82 354) can provide information. Kritsia is served by 12 buses daily from Agios Nikolaos (15mins, 230 dr).

I'm ready for my close-up, Mr De Mille

If the villagers seem to be preening before your camera, it's because they've had practice. In 1956, the American director Jules Dassin (*Never On Sunday*) chose Kritsa as the backdrop for *He Who Must Die*, the film version of Katzantzakis' novel *Christ Recrucified* starring Dassin's wife, Melina Mercouri. The film lovingly captured the worn faces of the villagers, many of whom acted in the film.

The telegenic village of Kritsa: whitewashed houses with a mountain backdrop

Neil Setchfield

RETHYMNO (4)

Blessed with a town beach and a wonderful old Venetian-Ottoman quarter (see p. 30), Rethymno is Crete's third-largest town. A late-Minoan tomb excavated in the south of the town and Roman mosaics within the town indicate that modern Rethymno is on the site of the ancient city of Rithymna.

The city flourished under the Venetians who made it an important commercial centre and built the fortress above the harbour. The city's artistic and intellectual heritage also dates to the Venetian era, when the schools of Rethymno led the way in philosophy and mathematics.

Today, it is home to the Faculty of Arts of the University of Crete. Rethymno was heavily bombed during WWII but its 12km-long beach has spurred a flurry of new construction along the shore.

Archaeological Museum (4, E4)

The museum contains artefacts from the Neolithic to the Roman periods, labelled in English and arranged chronologically. The exhibits include excavations from the Amari valley, the cemetery of Armeni and Elephtherna in the foothills of Mt Ida. The unfinished statue of Aphrodite from Lappa (Argiroupolis) was put together by joining several statue fragments found in 1910 and 1964. ✉ **opposite the fortress entrance** ☎ **0831-23 653** ⏱ **Tues-Sun 8.30am-3pm** 💲 **500 dr**

Historical & Folk Art Museum (4, G4)

If you have a Cretan grandmother, her attic might contain a lot of the items on display here. Old clothes and jewellery, kitchen supplies, farm implements, photos and country craftwork recreate the traditional Cretan lifestyle. ✉ **Vernardou 30** ☎ **0831-23 398** ⏱ **Mon-Sat 10am-2pm** 💲 **400 dr**

Rethymno Beach (4, H7)

The wide, sandy beach and clear water makes swimming a delight, but you won't be alone. The coast is marred by a string of hotels and the beach is jammed with lounge chairs and umbrellas as soon as the weather turns mild. ✉ **along Venizelou**

Stretch out along Rethymno's long, sandy town beach

Neil Setchfield

Pandelis Prevelakis

Iraklio has Kazantzakis but Rethymno has Prevelakis. The writer and poet Pandelis Prevelakis was born in Rethymno in 1908. He painted an exquisite portrait of his birthplace in his book *The Tale of a Town*. One of the most moving passages of the book deals with the expulsion of the Turkish community of Rethymno in 1923 after the failed Greek invasion of Smyrna. Riots broke out as Greek refugees from Smyrna waited to move into homes that the anguished Turks were destroying. Prevelakis is renowned as a poet and for his critical writings on Kazantzakis.

BEACHES

Crete has mastered the sun, sea and sand formula. Elafonisi (p. 19) is a favourite, but there are beaches for everyone's taste: tranquil, isolated spots; crowded, developed beaches; and striking, picturesque stretches of sand and water.

Very few beaches have any natural shade. The most you'll find is a few pine trees or palms. Nevertheless, you'll invariably find a concession on the beach renting umbrellas and lounge chairs for about 1500 dr for two people.

Generally you'll find south-coast beaches are much more deserted than north-coast beaches but the south is more subject to ripping winds in July and August. All beaches are more crowded on weekends when Cretans also head for the water.

Agia Galini (2, F7)
The steep, winding streets of this town on the sea have been over-colonised with shops, cafes and restaurants but maintain a certain allure. The beach is unimpressive but there are boat trips to other beaches and it makes an excellent base to visit Phaestos, Gortyn and Agia Triada.
⊠ 62km southeast of Rethymno ⌦ in peak season 8 buses daily to Iraklio (2½hrs, 1500 dr) and 4 to Rethymno (1½hrs, 1300 dr)

Bali (2, D7)
Bali has one of the most stunning settings on the north coast. No less than 5 little coves are strung along the indented shore, marked by hills, promontories and narrow, sandy beaches. The landscape is best appreciated from the water so try to rent a boat or paddleboat to get the full effect of the dramatic backdrop.
⊠ 38km east of Rethymno ⌦ buses between Iraklio and Rethymno drop you at the main road

Falassarna (2, D2)
Falassarna was a city-state in the 4th century BC but there's not much to see of it now. Most people head to Falassarna for its superb beach, which is long and sandy and interspersed with boulders.
⊠ 16km west of Kastelli-Kissamos
⌦ 2 buses daily from Kastelli-Kissamos (30mins, 600 dr) as well as buses from Hania (1hr, 1500 dr)

Hrysi Islet (2, G12)
Just a short jaunt over the sea from Ierapetra, Hrysi islet offers good, uncrowded, sandy beaches on a desert island. When the sun gets too intense you can wander into the lovely cedar forest on the island.
⊠ south of Ierapetra
⚲ excursion boat from Ierapetra (5000 dr return)

Kalamaki (2, F8)
The wide, sandy beach stretches for many km in either direction, giving you a rare opportunity for a long walk along a beach. Tourism is in its embryonic stage in Kalamaki after the recent opening of a paved road all the way to the beach.
⊠ 7km north of Matala ⌦ 1 daily bus from Iraklio via Mires (2hrs, 1550 dr)

Matala beach's caves – originally Roman tombs

Chris Christo

Matala (2, F8)

When you see the eerie caves speckling the rock slab on the beach's edge, you'll know why 1960s hippies found it like groovy, man. Joni Mitchell was among a number of hippies who lived in the caves; she wrote about the Matala moon in her song *Carey*. The caves were originally Roman tombs cut out of the sandstone rock in the 1st century AD.

✉ **70km southwest of Iraklio 🚌 5 buses daily from Iraklio (2hrs, 1500 dr)**

Paleohora (2, F2)

Laid-back Paleohora is the only beach resort on Crete that doesn't go into total hibernation in winter. The little town lies on a narrow peninsula with a long, curving sandy beach exposed to the wind on one side and a sheltered pebbly beach on the other. See page 63 for details of the beautiful coastal walk between Paleohora and Sougia.

✉ **77km southwest of Hania 🚌 in summer, 3 buses daily to Hania (2hrs, 1450 dr); in winter 2 buses daily. An extra daily service takes the back roads through mountain villages (3hrs). 🚢 the boat *Elafonisos* goes to the west-coast beach of Elafonisi (1hr, 1300 dr; see page 19); in summer, there are daily ferries from Paleohora to Hora Sfakion (3hrs, 3700 dr) via Sougia**

Plakias (2, F6)

The south-coast town of Plakias was once a tranquil retreat for adventurous backpackers – until the

package-tour operators discovered the fine beaches and dramatic mountain backdrop. Although the town has sprouted too many hotels, it's still an excellent place to escape the commercialism of north-coast beaches.

✉ **41km south of Rethymno 🚌 4 buses daily to Rethymno (1hr, 950 dr)**

Sweetwater (2, F4)

Named after fresh-water springs which seep from the rocks, this beach is beautiful – you won't be able to resist a swim in the translucent sea.

✉ **4km west of Hora Sfakion 🚢 coastal walk or taxi boat (4000 dr) from Hora Sfakion**

Vaï (2, D15)

Vaï is so famous for its palm forest that tourists arrive by the busload all summer. One theory about the palms' origins is that they sprouted from date pits spread by Roman legionaries relaxing on their way back from conquering Egypt. However, while the palms are closely related to the date palm, they are a separate species found only on Crete.

✉ **24km east of Sitia 🚌 5 buses daily from Sitia (1hr, 600 dr)**

Palm trees, umbrellas and bodies line Vaï beach.

Neil Setchfield

ANCIENT SITES

Wandering around the sites of Europe's oldest civilisation is an enduring attraction. Apart from the famous Minoan cities of Knossos, Gortyn, Phaestos and Zakros (see the Highlights chapter) there are plenty more sites, both Roman and Minoan, to visit.

Ancient archaeological sites can be difficult to appreciate. Often, little is left but neatly laid-out piles of stones, the bases of pillars or the beginnings of an impressive staircase. A good map of the sites helps but even more indispensable is a vivid imagination. The large area covered by the site can help you visualise the immensity of the palace or city; intersecting rows of stones trace passages or roads; wide staircases and massive columns hint at grandeur. The desolate, windswept locations of these sites also create the sense of uncovering secret civilisations.

The following sites are less famous so you'll be away from the tourist track and experiencing more authentic village life on the way.

Agia Triada (2, F8)

Agia Triada is a small Minoan site easily reached on foot from Phaestos (p. 29). Its principal building was smaller than the other royal palaces but built to a similar design. The opulence of the objects found at the site indicate that it was a royal residence, possibly a summer palace of Phaestos' rulers.

✉ 3km west of

Phaestos ⓘ 0892-91 360 ⬛ follow the signed road from the parking at Phaestos ⏱ 8.30am-3pm ⑤ 500 dr

Gournia (2, E12)

Dating from 1550-1450BC, Gournia's palace was less ostentatious than those at Knossos and Phaestos; it was the residence of an overlord rather than a king. The town is a network of streets and stairways flanked by houses. Trade, domestic and agricultural implements found indicate that Gournia was a thriving little community.

✉ 18km southeast of Agios Nikolaos ⓘ 0841-24 943 ⬛ Gournia is on the Sitia and Ierapetra bus routes from Agios Nikolaos; ask to be dropped at the site ⏱ Tues-Sun 8.30am-3pm ⑤ 500 dr

Lato (2, E12)

Founded in the 7th century BC by the Dorians, Lato was one of Crete's most powerful cities. It sprawls over the slopes of two acropolises in a lonely mountain setting, with stunning views of the Gulf of Mirabello.

✉ 13km southwest of Agios Nikolaos ⬛ 12 buses daily from Agios Nikolaos to Kritsa (15mins, 230 dr); stop 1km before Kritsa then walk 3km to site. ⬛ take the road to Kritsa and follow the

The 3500-year-old foundations of Gournia

Neil Setchfield

signs from the main
road ⊘ **Tues-Sun
8.30am-3pm ⑤ free**

Malia (2, E11)

The palace at Malia was
the third most important in
Minoan Crete, after
Knossos and Phaestos.
What we see here are
remains of the new palace
which was begun around
1650BC and destroyed by
fire about 200 years later.
The highlight is an unusual
kernos offering-slab with
24 depressions around the
edge. Its exact purpose is
unknown.

✉ **34km east of Iraklio**
ⓘ **0897-31 597** 🚌 **any
bus along the north
coast to/from Iraklio
can drop you at Malia**
⊘ **Tues-Sun 8.30am-
3pm ⑤ 800 dr**

Polyrrinia (2, D2)

It's a steep climb to the
ruins but the views are
stunning. The city was

Lato: lonely mountain setting and spectacular sea views

founded by the Dorians
and was continuously
inhabited until Venetian
times. There are remains of
city walls and an aqueduct
built by Hadrian.

✉ **7km south of**

Kastelli-Kissamos 🚌 **2
buses daily from
Kastelli-Kissamos in
winter and Mon, Wed,
Fri in summer (25mins,
400 dr)** ⊘ **daily ⑤
free**

After Knossos and Phaestos, the palace at Malia was the next most important in Minoan Crete.

VENETIAN & BYZANTINE LEGACIES

There are wonderful reminders of Crete's time in the Venetian and Byzantine empires. The old quarters of Hania (p. 26) and Rethymno (p. 30) are magnificent, while there are plenty of amazing fortresses and monasteries scattered around the island, many in stunning positions. Many of the monasteries contain fine examples of the frescoes and icons that are a hallmark of Cretan art. The interchange between Crete and Venice allowed some of the best aspects of Venetian architectural style to influence Crete, lending the churches and monasteries an austere elegance.

Church of Panagia Kera (2, E12)

Gracing the interior of this tiny triple-aisled church are frescoes that are considered the most outstanding examples of Byzantine art on Crete.

✉ 10km southwest of Agios Nikolaos, 1km before Kritsa ☎ 0841-51 525 🚌 12 buses daily from Agios Nikolaos (15mins, 230 dr) ◷ Mon-Sat 9am-3pm, Sun 9am-2pm Ⓢ 500 dr

Moni Arkadiou

(2, E7) This 16th-century monastery with an impressive Venetian baroque church stands in attractive hill country. Its striking façade (featured on the 100 dr note) has 8 slender Corinthian columns and is topped by an ornate triple-belled tower.

✉ 25km southeast of Rethymno 🚌 4 buses daily from Rethymno (30mins, 500 dr) ◷ 8am-1pm, 3.30-8pm Ⓢ free (museum 700 dr)

Moni Hrysoskalitissas

(2, E2) Inhabited by 2 nuns, this beautiful monastery is on a rock above the sea. Hrysoskalitissas means 'golden staircase', from a legend which claims that one of the 90 steps from the sea is made of gold.

✉ 73km southwest of Hania 🚌 buses to Elafonisi drop passengers here ◷ Tues-Sun 8.30am-3pm Ⓢ free

A Cretan Masada

In November 1866 the Turks sent massive forces to quell insurrections that were gathering momentum throughout the island. Hundreds of men, women and children who had fled their villages used the Arkadiou monastery as a safe haven. When 2000 Turkish soldiers staged an attack on the building, rather than surrender, the Cretans set fire to a store of gun powder. The explosion killed everyone, Turks included, except one small girl. This sole survivor lived to a ripe old age in a nearby village. A bust of this woman, and the abbot who lit the gun powder, stand outside the monastery.

Sacrificial site: Moni Arkadiou

Neil Setchfield

CRETE FOR CHILDREN

Cretans adore children and, with the island's many beaches, there's always somewhere to take the kids. Perhaps because of the ever-appealing sand and sea, amusement parks for kids are in short supply. Available options are listed here but don't forget that ruined Minoan palaces and ancient sites can be a make-believe wonderland for kids. They'll probably find it easier to conjure up vanished civilisations than you will, and they're usually eligible for discounts.

Dimotikos Kipos Public Garden (5, J9)

If your 5-year-old has lost interest in Hania's Venetian architecture before the end of the first street, head to the public gardens, where there's a playground, a small zoo with a resident *kri-kri* (Cretan wild goat) and a children's resource centre that has a small selection of books in English.
🕐 8am-11pm ⑤ free

Kritiki Farma

This recreation of a typical Cretan farm may be a little corny for adults but kids are sure to appreciate the carriage rides, donkey rides and playground. There's also a sampling of farm animals to help city kids connect pork and pig, as well as a restaurant serving Cretan dishes.
✉ Potamies (2, E10), 34km southeast of Iraklio ☎ 0897-51 546 🚌 from Iraklio there are 2 buses daily (except weekends) to Lassithi (2hrs, 1400 dr) and 3 buses daily (except weekends) returning to Iraklio 🕐 Mar-Oct 9am-7pm ⑤ 1500 dr (adults & children)

Limnoupolis Water Park (2, D4)

This splash park, larger than Water City (see below), has slides, spa and playground.
✉ Varipetro, 8km south of Hania ☎ 0821-33 224 🚌 regular buses from Hania in summer 🕐 Apr-Sept 10am-7pm ⑤ 3500/2500 dr

Water City (2, E10)

When the kids get tired of building sandcastles, take them here for 23 water slides, wave pools and an artificial river. On some slides, kids plunge from the heights while in others they emerge from a tube.
✉ 15km southeast of Iraklio ☎ 081-781 316 🚌 take the main road east from Iraklio and turn south at Chani Kokini, following signs to the park. 🕐 Apr-Sept 10am-7pm ⑤ 4000/3000 dr (children 4-12)

Crete offers plenty of souvenirs for younger visitors.

Leaving the Kids

Kids are welcome in any eating establishment but if you want to get away for an evening you may have a problem. Only the top-rung luxury hotels offer babysitting services. In lesser establishments you may be able to persuade the manager of the hotel to organise child-minding. Watch out for the hotel swimming pools – none of them are fenced.

OFF THE BEATEN TRACK

Getting away from tourists is easy – head inland. With most tourists clustered along the coast, much of the Cretan interior is practically deserted. It's helpful to have your own wheels so you can set your own pace and experience a rural lifestyle that has remained unchanged for centuries. The southern coast is less travelled than the northern coast and the eastern half of the island gets fewer visitors than the western half.

Ano Viannos (2, F11)
This delightful village on the southern flanks of Mt Dikti has an interesting folklore museum and the Church of Agios Pelagia, with fine frescoes by Nikoforos Fokas.

✉ **42km west of Mirtos** 🚌 **2 weekly buses to Iraklio (2½hrs, 1900 dr) and 2 to Ierapetra (1hr, 800 dr) via Mirtos** 🚗 **take the main road that runs between Iraklio and Ierapetra**

Margarites (2, E7)
Known for its fine pottery (p. 75), this tiny town is invaded by tour buses in the morning but by the afternoon all is calm and you can enjoy wonderful views over the valley from the taverna terraces on the main square.

✉ **27km southeast of Rethymno** 🚌 **Mon-Fri 2 buses daily from Rethymno (30mins, 600 dr)**

Mirtos (2, F12)
A sparkling, charming village of whitewashed houses with flower-filled balconies, Mirtos also has a decent sand and pebble beach.

✉ **48km southwest of Agios Nikolaos** 🚌 **6 buses daily from Ierapetra to Mirtos (30mins, 320 dr)** 🚗 **take the main road west from Ierapetra (16km)**

Omalos (2, E3)
Most tourists only hurry through Omalos on their way to the Samaria Gorge, but this plateau town deserves more. The air is bracingly cool in comparison with the sweltering coast in summer and there are some great mountain walks in the area. After the morning Samaria rush, there's hardly anyone on the plateau except goats and shepherds.

✉ **36km south of Hania** 🚌 **4 buses daily from Hania (1hr, 1250 dr)**

Go inland to talk to the goats

Spili (2, E6)
This gorgeous mountain town with cobbled streets, rustic houses and plane trees is beginning to attract more tourists. The highlight, in the town centre, is a Venetian fountain spurting water from 19 lion heads.

✉ **30km south of Rethymno** 🚌 **4 buses daily on the Rethymno-Agia Galini route (40mins, 340 dr)**

Spili's spurting fountain

Xerokambos (2, E15)
This tiny village, on the next bay south of Kato Zakros, is an unspoilt haven near several coves of inviting pale sand.

✉ **65km southeast of Sitia** 🚗 **from Sitia, take the main road to Ziros and follow signs to Xerokambos**

Zaros (2, F8)
If the name rings a bell, it's probably because your bottles of mineral water are labelled 'Zaros'. Known for its spring water and bottling plant right outside town, this is a traditional town where many people still wear black. Ask at the Hotel Idi (p. 105-6) about treks to local monasteries.

✉ **46km southwest of Iraklio** 🚌 **3 buses daily from Iraklio** 🚗 **take the main road south from Iraklio and turn west at Agia Varvara**

QUIRKY CRETE

Lepers, human sacrifice, cave-dwelling rebels and massacres were as much a part of Crete's tortured history as palaces and churches. The sights listed here will give you a glimpse of some of the grislier aspects of island life and, except for Spinalonga, you won't be running into many other tourists along the way. For a cheerier picture, head out to Milia to see what enterprising modern Cretans can do.

Melidoni Cave

(2, D7) Did the God Talos curse this cave because Medea killed him here? From the grisly events in 1824, one could think so. Over 300 villagers took refuge in the cave against the Turkish army, so the Turks threw burning materials through a hole in the top of the cave and everyone was asphyxiated. After paying homage to the martyrs at a monument, you can wander through a series of chambers filled with stalactites and stalagmites.
✉ **5km northeast of Perama, 21km east of Rethymno** 🚌 **Mon-Fri 2 buses daily from Rethymno to Anogia, stop at Perama (35mins, 460 dr)**

Milia (2, E2)

A few years ago, the only 2 families left in this isolated village managed to persuade the EU to help them reconstruct the village in its original style using traditional materials and furnish it with Cretan antiques. The rebuilt stone houses are occasionally rented out to Cretans or tourists who are looking for total isolation in a stunning mountain setting and don't mind the lack of electricity. There's also a traditional Cretan kitchen turning out scrumptious dishes from the

No Cemeteries

The Cretan diet rewards islanders with an extremely long life, but from the lack of visible cemeteries you might think they had achieved immortality. Not quite. Land is just too valuable to be reserved for the dearly departed. After 3 years, bones are removed from the burial ground and placed in a charnel house along with those of their ancestors.

organic produce in the village garden.
✉ **57km southwest of Hania** ☎ **0822-51 569** 🚌 **take the Elafonisi bus to Vlatos and follow the signs 5km to Milia** 🚗 **drive to Vlatos and watch for the turnoff to Milia. The rocky road between Vlatos and Milia is best suited to a 4WD.**

Military Museum

As you drive through Askifou, one sign after another directs you to the 'military museum', which turns out to be the gun and military odds-and-ends collection of Georgios Hatzidakis. The Sfakian is eager to show you around his collection, which includes various artefacts from this century's wars.

Diana Mayfield

War toys: the Military Museum in Askifou

Of Villages & Vampires

As though hazards like wars and vendettas weren't frightening enough, older Cretans believed they were also at threat from vampires, called *vrykolakas*. Suicides, unbaptised children and excommunicates could all become vrykolakas. Every night but Saturday, these flesh-eating ghouls allegedly roamed the hills searching for victims in remote mountain villages. Villagers said that if the vampire's blood touched you it would burn through your skin. The only way vrykolakas could achieve final rest was by being struck by lightning or consumed by fire.

✉ **Askifou** (2, E5)
☎ 0825-695 289
🚌 **Askifou is on the main road from Hania to Hora Sfakion. The bus will drop you off in town** ☉ **usually Mon-Sat 8am-7pm** ⑤ **free**

Sendoni Cave (2, E8)
Whether named after a rebel or a robber — according to local legends — Sendoni is the most spectacular cave on Crete. Stalactites, stalagmites and strange rock formations make the visit an eerie experience. The front of the cave was a hideout for Greek fighters against the Turks but most of the large cave was undisturbed. Walkways make exploration easier but it's still important to watch your step.
✉ **near Zoriana, 51km southeast of Rethymno**

🚌 **Mon-Fri 2 buses daily from Rethymno (1hr, 1000 dr)**

Spinalonga Island (2, D12) Known as 'the island of the dead', Spinalonga is a former leper colony and a fascinating day trip from Agios Nikolaos. The cemetery, with its open graves, is especially strange. Dead lepers came in 3 classes: those who had saved their government pension for a concrete box; those whose relations bought them a proper grave; and the destitute, whose remains were thrown into a charnel house. The last leper died in 1953 and the island has been uninhabited since.
✉ **just north of the Spinalonga Peninsula**
🚢 **regular excursion boats from Agios Nikolaos (2000 dr)**

Temple of Anemospilia
Human sacrifice is not commonly associated with the peace-loving Minoans but the evidence found at this site was irrefutable. In the 1980s scientists found 3 skeletons in positions indicating that a young man lying on an altar was bound and stabbed by 2 others, most likely a priestess and an assistant. The sacrifice was probably made just as the 1700BC earthquake began, in a desperate attempt to appease the gods. The site is now fenced but the scenic drive here makes it worthwhile.
✉ **2km northwest of Arhanes (2, E9), 17km south of Iraklio**
🚌 **bus from Iraklio (30mins, 340 dr)**

Roadside shrines mark victims of treacherous driving.

Neil Setchfield

KEEPING FIT

Active travellers will find a lot to keep them busy in Crete, whether it's swimming and windsurfing off the many beaches or horse-riding, trekking and biking through the interior. Follow with a relaxing session in a spa.

Cycling & Mountain-Biking

To reach remote beaches and monasteries, nothing beats having your own wheels. However, the mountainous interior can make cycling a challenge for all but the most experienced riders and the north coast is too traffic-heavy to be relaxing. Several companies have come up with the ideal solution: they transport you by bus to the top of a hill and allow you to pedal down, enjoying the spectacular scenery. In the west try Trekking Plan (see Hiking) and for those exploring the east there's Diexdos (☎ 0841-28 098). See also Organised Tours (p. 66-7).

Gyms

Affluent young Cretans are starting to buff up in gyms but facilities are far from plentiful outside Iraklio. Gyms usually work with membership cards, which makes them impractical for visitors, but a number of luxury hotels have fitness centres and some are open to guests from outside the hotel. One of the most modern is the fitness centre at the Royal Mare Village (☎ 0897-250 25) in Hersonisos. Near Iraklio, the Candia Maris (☎ 081-314 632) in Ammoudara also has a fully equipped gym. Both health clubs offer aerobics, calisthenics etc. The cost is 5000 dr a day including use of a spa and sauna.

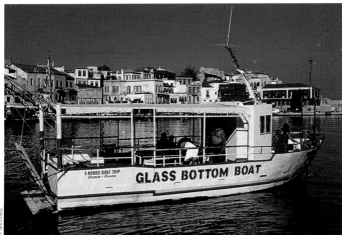

When it gets too hot to work out, take a pleasure cruise

Hiking

There are dozens of interesting hikes throughout Crete, taking you through remote villages, across plains and into gorges. You'll find a selection of the best hikes in the Out & About chapter (p. 57-63). If you'd like to go with a guided group, try The Happy Walker (☎ 0831-52 920), Tobazi 56 in Rethymno, or Trekking Plan (☎ 0821-60 861), in Agia Marina just outside Hania (p. 66-7).

Horse Riding

Travelling on horseback allows you to cover a good deal of territory in the countryside without working up a sweat. There's Horse Riding Club on the Akrotiri peninsula, east of Hania (☎ 0821-39 366); Melanouri Horsefarm in Pitsidia, near Matala (☎ 0892-45 040); and Finikia Stables a few km south of Iraklio (☎ 081-316 837). See also Organised Tours (p. 66-7).

Snorkelling & Diving

The warm, clear waters off Crete make snorkelling and diving a pleasure. Some of the best snorkelling is around the sunken city of Olous (2, E12) in Elounda (near Agios Nikolaos). In the shallow water you can see foundations of ancient houses.

A number of dive centres allow you to get acquainted with diving, become a certified diver or explore the underwater wonders if you're already certified. Under Greek law, you must dive as part of a licensed diving operation and you are forbidden to disturb any antiquities you may come across.

In Hania, you have a choice of Blue Adventures Diving (☎ 0821-40 608), Daskalogianni 69, or Creta's Diving Center (☎ 0821-93 616),

Samaria Gorge: a hiker's nirvana

John Elk III

Papanikoli 6 in Nea Hora. In Bali, there's Hippocampos (☎ 0834-94 193) near the port. In Agios Nikolaos, there's a diving centre affiliated with the aquarium (p. 35) and a diving centre on the beach of the Coral Hotel (☎ 0841-82 546). In Rethymno, there's the Paradise Dive Centre (☎ 0831-53 258), El Venizelou 76. It's wise to call at least a day in advance.

Swimming

Swimming is great all over the Cretan coast. Kids like the shallow waters off Falassarna, Elafonisi and Frangokastello, while serious swimmers may prefer the deeper waters of Rethymno, Matala, Sitia, Paleohora and other beaches. The water quality is very good – warm with no sharks. All beaches are public in Crete. Even if a large hotel blocks the way, you must be given access to the beach.

Water Sports

Parasailing, waterskiing, jet-skiing, pedal boating, canoeing and windsurfing are available on most of the major beaches. On the north coast, you'll find a water-sports centre attached to most luxury hotels and you don't need to stay there to avail yourself of the facilities. Outside Iraklio, try the water-sports centre at the Grecotel Agapi Beach (☎ 081-250 502) in Ammoudara. Outside Hania in nearby Platanias, there's Argiris Sea Sports (☎ 0821-093 493 449).

If you're staying in Agios Nikolaos, head out to the beach resort of Elounda, 12km north of town. There's a water-sports centre at the Elounda Bay hotel (☎ 0841-41 502) and the neighboring Elounda Beach hotel (☎ 0841-41 412). In Bali, there's the Water Sports Lefteris (☎ 0834-94 102) and in Vaï, there's Vaï Watersports (☎ 0843-61 070). Elafonisi, Falassarna, Xerokambos and Kato Zakros beaches have no water-sports centres yet.

The best windsurfing is at Kouremenos beach, the town beach of Palekastro, east of Sitia; contact the Kouremenos Water Sports Center (☎ 0843-093 751 7444). Windsurfing is also good in Paleohora. Try Westwind (☎ 0823-094 681 9777) near the Pal Beach hotel.

Pamperings

After you've finished climbing mountains and pedalling across plains you may be ready for something a little less energetic. **Thalassotherapy** (*thalassa* is the Greek word for 'sea') is just the right solution for aching muscles and psychic stresses. You can wrap yourself in mud and seaweed, get pummelled by water jets, inhale therapeutic steam and be massaged, then enjoy beauty treatments of various peelings and polishings.

The 2 most developed thalassotherapy centres are at the **Candia Maris hotel** and the **Royal Mare Village** (p. 53). A day of thalassotherapy at the Royal Mare is 26,000 dr; at the Candia Maris it's 24,000 dr. The Royal Mare is the newest and most luxurious facility, with hi-tech equipment and a vast thalasso pool. Both centres require you to see a staff doctor before beginning the program.

out & about

Whether you take a guided tour, rent your own wheels or rely on foot power, Crete offers a wealth of choices. The cities are rich in monuments, fortresses and fountains while the rugged interior is crisscrossed with hiking paths that take you up mountains, through gorges and across plains.

Signs of Trouble

One reason for the scarcity of road signs in Crete is that they tend to get shot up. On an island where most adult men have a firearm, road signs make irresistible targets for would-be marksmen. After a few hits by a rifle or .45 Magnum, piecing together the name on a sign is about as easy as deciphering Linear A.

Roads cut into coastal mountains and meander by country villages, alternating vistas of sea and sky with glimpses of centuries-old rural life.

How you choose to experience Crete will depend on your time, energy and budget, as well as the climate. Summers are hot, so if you choose to hike or tour the cities from June to August, get an early start. Most guided walks begin early and finish with lunch in a village taverna. The complicated network of paths and lanes that link interior villages makes walking with a guide an attractive option.

Road Safety

Fine weather and scenic mountain roads make motorcycling an attractive way to travel but you need to exercise extreme caution. Country roads can be in poor condition, with giant potholes and loose gravel. Even good roads can suddenly degenerate without warning just as you're zipping along admiring the scenery. Renting a moped is much safer since you'll be forced to keep a safe speed. Rental outlets are everywhere and a basic model costs about 4000 dr a day. If you will be riding 2 to a bike, make sure your model has enough horsepower to get both of you up the hills.

Road Signs & Maps

If you explore the island by car or scooter, prepare to spend a fair amount of time poring over maps, since country roads are often unmarked. Road signs, when they exist, are usually in both Greek and Latin letters except in remote locations. Even when written in Latin letters, the spelling of place names can vary wildly from the names on your map or in this book. Invest in a good map (Road Editions publishes the most accurate Crete map), but even the best maps don't cover all the side roads.

Zippy local transport

Neil Setchfield

WALKING TOURS
Hania's Old Quarter

Begin at the covered food market **(1)** on Plateia Hortatson. For the full market experience, try to be there in the morning, Monday to Saturday. Go around behind the municipal market to Tsouderon. Take a look at the minaret **(2)**, one of only 2 left in Hania. Turn left on Tsouderon and continue until it turns into Skridlof, aka Leather Lane, with its rows of leather shops. You'll soon come to Halidon, the main shopping street. Across the street is the Schiavo Bastion **(3)**.

Turn right on Halidon and you'll come to the Folklore Museum **(4)** and then the Archaeological Museum **(5)** on your left. Grab a bite to eat at *Cafe Eaterie Ekstra* **(6)**, nearby at Zambeliou 8. Continue on to Plateia Venizelou with the Mosque of the Janissaries **(7)** on the right.

Retrace your steps and stroll

Walk on in: the Archaeological Museum

distance 5km **duration** 2hrs
start food market
end Venetian Arsenal

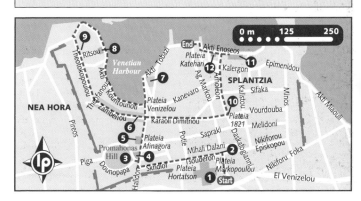

SIGHTS & HIGHLIGHTS

Food market (p. 36)
Minaret
Schiavo Bastion
Folklore Museum
Archaeological Museum (p. 36)
Mosque of the Janissaries (p. 36-7)
Naval Museum (p. 37)
Turkish houses
Plateia 1821
Venetian Arsenal

Turkish Houses

Turkish houses are distinguished by timber awnings jutting out from the building on the 1st and 2nd floors. During the time of Turkish rule it was believed that Muslim women needed to be 'protected' from the rapacious glances of men and thus they were kept imprisoned in the house. The timber protrusions allowed women to gaze out onto the street without being seen by the men passing below.

along the inner harbour. You'll notice a wealth of Venetian townhouses, all attractively restored, along the harbourfront. At the end of the harbour is the Naval Museum **(8)**.

Trek around the promontory and turn left up Theotokopoulou, which has roofless Venetian buildings turned into pleasant outdoor restaurants. Notice the restored Turkish houses at Lena's Pension **(9)**. Turn left at Zambeliou and cross Halidon, continuing straight along Karaoli Dimitriou until you come to the shady Plateia 1821 **(10)** and the Agios Nikolaos church. There are several cafes on this relaxing square.

Turn left on Daskalogianni, which becomes Arholeon; as you head to the sea you'll come upon the 16th-century Venetian Arsenal **(11)** on your right. It is now cafes and exhibition spaces.

You can have a drink at the trendy *Four Seasons* **(12)** and then turn right to stroll along the east harbour or turn left to go back to Halidon.

Hania's glorious Venetian harbour

Neil Setchfield

Iraklio Stroll

Begin at the Archaeological Museum **(1)**, Crete's top attraction, and after your visit head to Plateia Eleftherias **(2)**. Take the pedestrian shopping street, Dedalou, to Plateia Venizelou and stop for a spot of people-watching around the Morosini fountain **(3)**. Turn right on 25 Avgoustou and on your right you'll see the Agios Markos church **(4)**. Further along on the right is the Venetian loggia **(5)**, now used for art exhibitions. Turn right at the loggia and you'll come to the Agios Titos church **(6)**, built by the Venetians, turned into a mosque by the Turks and then converted into an Orthodox church after Turkish rule ended.

Head back to 25 Avgoustou and continue towards the harbour. Cross S Venizelou and walk along the sea wall to the fortress **(7)**. Walk back to S Venizelou and take a break at *Ippokampos Ouzeri* **(8)**, at Mitsotaki 2. Continue west along S Venizelou to the Historical Museum **(9)**.

Go up Grevenon to Plateia El Venizelou. Cross Dikeosynis onto the

distance 7km **duration** 4hrs
start Archaeological Museum
end Church of Agia Ekaterini

Plateia Eleftherias (top) and the Agios Titos church (bottom)

Agios Minos Cathedral

SIGHTS & HIGHLIGHTS

Archaeological Museum (p. 16-17)
Plateia Eleftherias
Morosini Fountain (p. 41)
Venetian loggia
Agios Titos church
Rocca al Mare fortress (p. 41)
Historical Museum (p. 41)
Bembo Fountain (p. 40)
Jesus Bastion
Kazantzakis' Tomb (p. 41)
Agios Minos Cathedral
Icon Museum, Church of Agia Ekaterini (p. 40)

market street, 1866, and walk south. If you're ready for some food, stop at *Giakoumis* **(10)** on Theodosaki. Then continue on 1866 to the Venetian-built Bembo fountain **(11)**.

Make a left and then a right on Evans. Continue to Plastira and make a right. You'll be walking along the walls, passing first Jesus Bastion **(12)**. On your left you'll then come to Nikos Kazantzakis's tomb **(13)** on the Martinengo Bastion.

Continue in the same direction on Plastira, turn right on Gianikou and you come to Plateia Arkadiou. Turn left and walk to Agios Minos Cathedral **(14)**.

On the other end of the plateia is the former church of Agia Ekaterini, now an icon museum **(15)** featuring works from the 'Cretan Renaissance' including 6 by Mihail Damaskinos.

The Venetian loggia: art inside and out

Samaria Gorge Hike

The trek begins at **Xyloskalo**, the steep wooden staircase that gives access to the Samaria Gorge. The towering wall of rock on the right is **Mt Gingilos** (2, E3). You'll descend swiftly – about 1km in the first 2km of the walk – but the route levels out after the **chapel of Agios Nikolaos** on the right. The abandoned **village of Samaria** signals the halfway point. The warden's office is in the abandoned village and just south is a **small church** dedicated to Saint Maria of Egypt, after whom the gorge is named.

distance 18km **duration** 6hrs
start 🚌 bus to Xyloskalo from Hania
end ⛴ boat from Agia Roumeli to Hora Sfakion
ⓘ visitor centre at Xyloskalo

The walk becomes rockier and the scenery more spectacular as the rock walls rise majestically on either side. The path narrows until, at the 12km mark, the walls are only 3.5m apart – the famous **Iron Gates**. After a few more kms you'll reach the almost abandoned village of Old Agia Roumeli where there are stands selling overpriced drinks. The last km is the dullest but finally you arrive at the small resort of **Agia Roumeli**, where you can grab some lunch at *Kri Kri* restaurant or wade into the sparkling sea.

For more information on Samaria Gorge, see page 31.

The Samaria Gorge hike begins with a swift descent.

Neil Setchfield

Lassithi Plateau Walk

This 90-minute walk from Tzermiado to Psyhro goes through the heart of the Lassithi plateau, replete with fields of onions, wheat, cabbage, beans and kale. If you're lucky, the famous **windmills** will be unfurled and pumping water to irrigate the fields. Even if the windmills are idle, it's a lovely walk.

John Pendlebury

From the centre of Tzermiado, it's easy to follow signs to the Trapeza Cave, a Neolithic burial site excavated by the Indiana Jones of Cretan archaeology – John Pendlebury.

Pendlebury was a protegé of Sir Arthur Evans who, impressed by his brilliance and physical endurance, made him curator of Knossos. In addition to his administrative duties, Pendlebury produced a layman's guide to Knossos (available in the site's bookstore) and tramped through Crete searching out other possible sites. He began excavations of Trapeza Cave and another site in 1936 but war interrupted his work.

Pendlebury immediately enlisted and was put in charge of coordinating the Cretan resistance. His knowledge of the countryside was put to good use as he hiked the hills in traditional Cretan dress with a rifle over his shoulder and a patch over his eye. Cretans loved him.

During the Battle of Crete in May 1941, Pendlebury fought heroically against German parachutists but was wounded. While he was waiting for a doctor in a house near Iraklio, German soldiers entered and shot him.

> **distance** 7km **duration** 1½hrs
> **start** 🚌 2 buses daily to Tzermiado from Iraklio
> **end** 🚌 3 buses daily from Psyhro to Iraklio (last one at 4.15pm)

From Tzermiado's central square take the street with the Agricultural Bank and OTE. At the end, turn right, and then take the first left onto a road which becomes a dirt track. Continue ahead for 1km, turn right at the T-junction, and then veer right onto the surfaced road. At the cross-roads, turn left onto a rough dirt track. Turn right at the second crossroads and you will see **Psyhro** (2, E11) in the distance to the left. Continue straight ahead for 1km, and turn left at the T-junction. At the road, turn left to reach Psyhro's central square. If you're hungry, you face the agonising choice between *Stavros* or *Platanos* tavernas – the only dining establishments in town. Continue straight ahead from the town square to reach the **Dikteon Cave** (2, E11).

See also pages 24-5.

Hilltop church, Lassithi

Neil Setchfield

Paleohora-Sougia Coastal Walk

From Paleohora's town centre, follow signs to the camping grounds to the northeast. Turn right at the intersection with the road to Anidri and soon you'll be following the coastal path marked as the E4 European Footpath.

After a couple of km, the path climbs steeply for a beautiful view back to Paleohora. You'll pass **Anidri beach** and several inviting **coves** where people may be getting an all-over tan. Take a dip because the path soon turns inland to pass over **Cape Flomes**. You'll walk along a plateau carpeted with brush that leads toward the coast and some breathtaking views over the Libyan Sea. Soon you'll reach the Minoan site of **Lissos** (2, F3).

After Lissos the path takes you through a pine forest and then a **gorge** bedecked with oleander and studded with some perfect picnic spots. The road ends at Sougia harbour. Since the walk is nearly shadeless it's important to take sunscreen and several litres of water. Between June and August, it's best to start at sunrise in order to get to Sougia before the heat of the day clamps down.

> **distance** 17km **duration** 4¾hrs
> **start** 🚌 daily buses to Paleohora from Hania (2hrs, 1450 dr); ⛴ summer ferries daily to Paleohora from Hora Sfakion (3hrs, 3700 dr) via Sougia (1hr, 950 dr)
> **end** 🚌 daily bus from Sougia to Hania (2½hrs, 1400 dr) at 1.30pm

For more information on Paleohora beach, see page 45.

Jeanne Oliver

Paleohora is the starting point for the walk, if you can drag yourself away.

DRIVING TOURS
Hania to the Samaria Gorge

The road from Hania **(1)** to the beginning of the Samaria Gorge is one of the most spectacular routes in Crete. The paved road is in good condition until Lakki, when hairpin-turns, potholes and goats obstruct smooth driving. The route heads through orange groves to the town of Fournes **(2)**, where a left fork leads to Meskla **(3)**. The main road continues to the village of Lakki **(4)**, 24km from Hania. The *Kri-Kri Restaurant & Rooms* has good-value meals. From Lakki, the road continues to the Omalos plateau **(5)** and Xyloskalo **(6)**, the start of the Samaria Gorge. Rather than eat at the expensive snack bar for tourists in Xyloskalo, try the friendly *Giglios* hotel-restaurant in Omalos.

For more information on Samaria Gorge, see page 31.

The postcard village of Lakki enjoys stunning views

Neil Setchfield

> **distance** 42km **duration** 1hr
> **start** Hania
> **end** Xyloskalo

For more information on Samaria Gorge, see page 31.

SIGHTS & HIGHLIGHTS

Fournes A good-sized town devoted to marketing the region's agricultural products

Meskla A serene village with a 14th-century chapel to the Panagia

Lakki A village perched on the edge of a valley that affords stunning views wherever you look

Omalos Plateau A vast empty plain where early spring floods are followed by a carpet of wildflowers (p. 50)

Xyloskalo The entrance to the Samaria Gorge (p. 61)

Agios Nikolaos to Sitia

The road from Agios Nikolaos **(1)** to Sitia takes you along the indented north-eastern coast, with splendid views over the sea to your left and the coastal mountains on your right.

Follow the road east past the beach resort of Istron **(2)**. In less than 10km you'll reach the Minoan site of Gournia **(3)**. Just after it is the beach town of Pahia Ammos **(4)**. The road climbs into the mountains to Platanos **(5)**, where you'll find the taverna *Panorama* (the name says it all) and picnic spots.

A few km after Platanos, there's a turn-off for a scenic, winding road to Mohlos **(6)**. Return to the main road, which is bordered with snow-white oleander, and continue past Mirsini **(7)**. You'll pass Messa Mouliana **(8)**, known for its wine, and Hamezi **(9)**. When you enter the village of Skopi **(10)**, watch for the turn-off on your right to Moni Faneromenis **(11)**. After your visit to the monastery, head back to the main road and continue on to Sitia.

Gournia A modest Minoan site (p. 46)

SIGHTS & HIGHLIGHTS

Istron A beach resort on a lovely cove
Gournia A modest Minoan site (p. 46)
Pahia Ammos Low-key beach mainly visited by locals
Platanos Small mountain village with sweeping coastal vistas
Mohlos Has rocky coves for swimming and an archaeological site undergoing excavation
Mirsini Pottery and weaving workshops plus a frescoed 14th-century chapel and great views
Hamezi Has a folklore museum and an unusual, oval-shaped ruin from the Minoan period
Moni Faneromenis A late-Byzantine monastery with stunning coastal views

Neil Setchfield

The inviting beach at Istron

distance 73km **duration** 2hrs
start Agios Nikolaos **end** Sitia
Excellent on the main road and partly paved on the road to Moni Faneromenis

ORGANISED TOURS

Whether you want to see the island by boat, bus, jeep, bicycle, foot or on horseback, there's an organised tour for you. Organised tours can take you to otherwise inaccessible spots without the hassles of buses, maps, bad roads, poor signposts, boat rentals or recalcitrant taxi drivers. The tour guide may provide fascinating insights into local culture and is there to answer questions. The disadvantages are that you are locked into a pre-scheduled itinerary and, if you have limited time, there may not be a tour going to your destination on the days when you are available.

Most agencies have a tour schedule: Monday to the Samaria Gorge, Tuesday to Knossos etc. In large towns such as Hania, Agios Nikolaos, Iraklio or Rethymno, travel agencies selling tours are abundant but they usually deal with one tour operator who provides the transport and guide. Price-shopping is useless since the prices are set by the tour operator. Most tours take children up to 4 years old for free and give a 50% discount to children between 5 and 15.

One of the most popular tours is to the **Samaria Gorge**, a trip you can arrange from almost any place on the island. The price ranges from 4500-9500 dr, depending on your starting point, but it does not include the admission fee to the gorge or the boat trip from Agia Roumeli to Hora Sfakion. Most agencies also offer a cheaper Samaria Gorge 'easy way' that takes you from Agia Roumeli to the Iron Gates. Unfortunately the route to the famous rock slabs is mostly hot and boring but you will get a sense of the gorge's majesty.

The Minoan palace of **Knossos** is another tour favourite but taking a tour makes little sense if you're staying in nearby Iraklio. From Hania or Agios Nikolaos a tour costs 7000-7500 dr and includes a guide, transport

---

Thar's gold in them thar' caves!

The islet off Gramvousa Peninsula is named *Imeri Gramvousa*, or Tame Gramvousa, but its role in Cretan history is anything but tame. The Venetians built a fortress here in 1579 and filled it with cannons and ammunition. When the Turks conquered Crete in 1648 the fort was left in Venetian hands until the Turks bribed the fort's commander in 1892 and took possession of it. In 1825 Cretan revolutionaries stormed the fortress, intending to use it as a base for their fight for independence. In order to support themselves they resorted to piracy. Before the Turks recaptured the island, the pirates amassed a fabulous fortune, which they reportedly hid in caves around the island. Who knows? It could still be there today.

Gramvousa islet: anything but tame

Chris Christo

and some free time for shopping and lunch in Iraklio. Admission to the site is not included.

If you want to get far off the beaten track, **4WD safaris** are a popular option. Although expensive (12,000-16,000 dr), you can reach delightfully out-of-the-way villages and sights. If the agency is sending out a procession of 4WDs however, your main sight will be the dust from the vehicle ahead. 4WD safaris generally include lunch in a local taverna.

Depending on your location you may be able to take tours to the Dikteon cave on the Lassithi plateau as well as the towns, sights and beaches of south Crete, east Crete and west Crete. There are also various **village tours** that lean heavily toward shopping during the day and dinner/folk-dancing shows at night. These tours can be worthwhile, especially if you have more money than time, but they can get crowded in summer. **Boat tours** with swimming included operate from the harbours of Hania, Rethymno and Agios Nikolaos as well as many south-coast beaches. These tours can also get crowded but, unless you have your own boat, an organised tour is the only way to see remote beaches and islands.

Below are some options for more unusual tours:

X & K Maritime Company
The tour (Apr-Oct) takes in the wild and remote Gramvousa Peninsula (inaccessible by car) and Gramvousa Island, a former pirates' lair. White-sand beaches, a climb to the top of a Venetian castle and the cove where Prince Charles and Diana reportedly honeymooned are also on the itinerary.
✉ **Port of Kastelli-Kissamos ☎ 0822-24 344/23 650 ⑤ 5000 dr**

Diexodos Adventure Unlimited
This company offers cycling tours that take in the Lassithi plateau and treks that include the archaeological site of Lato, Dikta summit and country villages. All tours leave from Kritsa.
✉ **Havania ☎ 0841-28098 ⑤ 14,000-16,000 dr for cycling trips; 12,000 dr for treks**

The Happy Walker
A minibus takes you from Rethymno to a mountain village which you use as a base to discover the region. Byzantine churches, country lanes, wildflowers and a taverna lunch are part of the program.
✉ **Tobazi 56, Rethymno ☎ 0831-52 920 ⑤ from 6500 dr, not including lunch**

Horse Riding Club
This informal establishment offers rides to the monasteries in the region as well beach rides and sunset rides.
✉ **Tersanas ☎ 0821-39 366 ⑤ 6000 dr for about 1½hrs; 12,000 dr for a half day**

Melanouri Horsefarm
These stables offer beach rides, moonlight rides and day-long tours of the region, including village visits and picnics.
✉ **Pitsidia, near Matala ☎ 0892-45 040**

⑤ **5000 dr for 1½hrs; 12,000 dr a day**

Trekking Plan
The company organises treks at all levels in the Lefka Ori as well as more demanding treks through the Aradena Gorge, the Agia Irini Gorge and the Imbros Gorge.
✉ **Agia Marina, next to the Santa Marina hotel ☎ 0821-60 861 ⑤ 8000-12,000 dr**

Fenny's Hania
Historian Tony Fennymore has a wealth of information about Hania's history and culture. During the season (Apr-Jul and Sept-Oct) his 2-hour walking tours begin at the `Hand' monument on Plateia Talo at the bottom of Theotokopoulou and end by the inner harbour. He also runs guided minibus tours around the region.
✉ **Theotokopoulou 3, Hania ☎ 0821-87 139 ⑤ 3500 dr**

shopping

Crete's long tradition of artisanship has mushroomed into a giant industry. Blue ceramics, clay pottery, handmade leather goods, woven rugs, icons, embroidered linen and finely wrought gold jewellery fill shops in all the tourist centres. In addition to crafted works there's also wild herbs, olive oil, sea sponges, Cretan wine, jellies, cheese, olives and other edible goodies.

Shopping with the family in Rethymno

Most of the products displayed in the ubiquitous souvenir stores are mass-produced. Although they can still be good value, it's worthwhile seeking out special shops that offer authentic Cretan items. Of all the large towns, you'll find the best selection of crafts in **Hania**. Maybe it's the beauty of the city's architecture that has inspired artisans, but you'll find the island's most artful leather, jewellery and rugs in the streets behind the harbour. **Rethymno** and **Agios Nikolaos** have a few good craft places but you have to plough through miles of souvenir shops. As the island's capital and richest city, **Iraklio** has more high-end stores for clothing, appliances and music but fewer souvenir and crafts shops. Several villages in the

Periptero

Cretan stores may have erratic opening hours but there's always a *periptero* to take up the slack. These convenient kiosks have long opening hours and sell newspapers, cigarettes, sweets, aspirin, razor blades, batteries, postcards, stamps, soap, condoms and shoelaces, among other necessities. They also have phones that usually work on a meter system although some take phonecards.

Souvenirs both traditional and touristy, from Hania

interior are known for their crafts. You can get good buys on linen in **Anogia** and **Kritsa** while spending a pleasant day tooling around the countryside.

Credit cards are accepted in city stores and in most of the larger village stores but you may get a slightly better price if you pay cash. It can't hurt to try bargaining, especially if you're buying in quantity, but don't expect major reductions. Larger stores will ship pottery, ceramics and other bulky items back home for you. Remember that you may be subject to duties on any item shipped to your home country.

VAT Refund

Greece tacks 13-18% VAT onto most consumer items which non-EU residents are entitled to recoup. The minimum purchase for a refund is 40,001 dr in a single store and the refund usually amounts to 15%. Participating stores will give you a refund form that must be filled out and presented to the refund officer at the point of departure from the EU. You must also present the receipt and the article purchased. A copy of the form is mailed back to the store which will send you a cheque or credit your credit card.

Opening Hours

Most stores open around 8am and close from about 1-5pm, reopening until 8 or 9pm. Stores are closed on Sunday and sometimes on Monday. Hours vary considerably but during the summer season many shops selling souvenirs and other tourist items are open 7 days.

Best Buys

Cassettes & CDs Portable and relatively inexpensive, recordings of Greek and Cretan music are easy to find. *Cretan Songs* by G Klados is a good compilation of songs played on lyra and lute.

Woven Goods Rugs, tapestries and handbags woven from cotton or wool are good value. Traditional Cretan designs are marked by strong colours, especially red.

Ceramics The shiny, dark-blue glaze of Cretan ceramics is easily distinguishable from the lighter matte finish of other Greek ceramics. The glaze should be hard enough not to scratch under the blade of a knife; a glazed bottom is the sign of machine-made pottery.

Leather The leather is hard rather than supple but reasonably priced nonetheless; durable bags, wallets, shoes and boots are best bought on 'Leather Lane' in Hania.

Jewellery You'll find more idiosyncratic pieces in silver than gold. Look for replicas of Minoan objects (such as the Phaestos disc) which are well crafted and available only on Crete.

Cretan ceramics: so blue

AGIOS NIKOLAOS

A certain crass commercialism persists in Agios Nikolaos, even though the tackiest enterprises have migrated to Malia and Hersonisos. The rows of identical souvenir sellers on **Koundourou** and **28 Oktovriou** testify to the enduring desire to make a fast buck from package tourism. The offerings run the gamut from cheap Asian imports to luxury watches but the bulk of the stores offer mid-range ceramics, icons, beach gear, light cotton clothing and postcards.

CRAFT, ART & ANTIQUES

Kerazoza (3, G3)
Kerazoza means `rainbow' in the Cretan dialect and refers to the shop's focus on make-believe and illusion. The unusual items include handmade masks, marionettes and figurines derived from ancient Greek theatre.
✉ **R. Koundourou 42** ☎ **0841-22 562** ○ **Mar-Jan 10am-10pm**

Maria Patsaki (3, H4)
In this eclectic store you'll

Retail therapy

find embroidery, rugs and antiques that are a cut above the average.
✉ **K. Sfakianaki 2** ☎ **0841-22 001** ○ **Mar-Oct 8am-10pm**

MUSIC & BOOKS

Anna Karteri (3, H3)
The English book selection here concentrates on bestsellers and books about Crete and Greece with plenty of glossy photos.
✉ **Koundourou 5** ☎ **0841-22 272** ○ **Mon-Sat 8am-10pm**

Panagiotis Eydaimon Music Formula (3, J2)
If the strange harmonies of Cretan and Greek music are bewitching you, here is where you can find a good selection of tapes and CDs.
✉ **Kontogianni 13** ☎ **0841-26 029** ○ **Apr-Oct Mon-Sat 8am-9pm; Nov-Mar Mon-Sat 8am-noon & 4-8pm**

Sea Sponges

By now there may be more sponges hanging in tourist shops than there are left in the Mediterranean. It's hard to believe that these cleaning aids are actually dead animals. Sponges are multicelled invertebrates that function as marine water filters, devouring micro-organisms in the water and expelling the remaining water from holes in their `heads'. Some sponges house crabs and other small animals, while others have become carnivorous, trapping and eating unwary organisms. Divers find the sponges off the Cretan coast, then boil and bleach them. If you're used to synthetic sponges, you'll find natural sponges pleasantly soft, absorbent and durable.

Harvested from the sea for your scrubbing pleasure

Neil Setchfield

HANIA

Now you're talking shopping. Hania offers the best combination of souvenir hunting and craft shopping on the island. The main street is **Halidon**, which is impossible to avoid since it connects the inner town with the harbour. There are no great shops on Halidon but there are several international bookshops and newsstands. The streets around Halidon are very touristy, offering souvenirs, photo supplies, postcards and the like. **El Venizelou** along the harbour has the odd gem hidden among the cafes. **Zambeliou, Theotokopoulou** and **Angelou** in the inner harbour are where the smaller, more interesting shops are. **Skridlof** is 'leather lane', with good quality handmade boots, sandals and bags. Feast your eyes on Hania's magnificent covered **food market** (5, G6); it makes all other food markets look like stalls at a church bazaar.

Angelou Street

CERAMICS & JEWELLERY
Carmela's Ceramic Shop (5, E3)
Carmela produces ceramics using ancient techniques and also displays unusual jewellery handcrafted by young Greek artisans.
✉ Angelou 7 ☎ 0821-90 487 ⏰ Mon-Sat 8am-8pm; Sun 8am-5pm

CRAFT, ART & ANTIQUES
Antiques Gallery
(5, E4) Most of the stuff here is, alas, too bulky to tuck into your suitcase. As well as framed paintings and old furniture, there are more unusual odds and ends dating to Hania's centuries under Turkish occupation.
✉ Akti Tobazi 1 ☎ 0821-0994 42 7070
⏰ 8am-9pm

Apostolos Pahtikos
(5, E6) Apostolos has been making traditional Cretan knives since he was 13, which was a very long time ago. You can watch him work as he matches the blade to the carefully carved handle.
✉ Sifaka 14 ⏰ Mon-Sat 10am-7pm

Hania District Association of Handicrafts Showroom (5, D5)
The embroidery, weaving and ceramics here are well-executed but the sculptures of Greek mythological figures are unusually fine. The showroom is appealingly devoid of sales pressure.
✉ Akti Tobazi 15 ☎ 0821-56 386 ⏰ Mon-Sat 9.30am-9pm; Sun 10.30am-5.30pm

Mount Athos (5, F4)
This glossy shop offers handmade icons but the best deals are on the handmade chess sets using figures from Greek mythology.
✉ Kondilaki 12 ☎ 0821-88 375 ⏰ Mon-Sat 8am-2pm & 5-9pm

Looking for a bag? Try Skridlof St, aka Leather Lane.

Knife Knowhow

Given the island's unruly history, it's not surprising that Cretans know their knives. Traditional Cretan dress for men always includes a knife, often white-handled, along with the standard black shirt, trousers and boots.

Knives have acquired a power that borders on the mystical. Older Cretans believe that knives made during Holy Week can protect you from evil spirits. In eastern Crete it's considered bad luck to give a knife as a present, while in western Crete it's considered good luck for the best man or godfather at a wedding to be presented with a knife.

Although the Minoans certainly produced knives, the current version probably developed under Turkish rule. At that time, the handles were made from buffalo horn or mountain-goat antler, but since horns have become scarcer cutlers sometimes use cattle bones. Unfortunately, the cutlers' craft is slowly disappearing, but you can always make your own knife. Here's how:

- If you don't have a goat horn, get a good slab of cattle bone
- Boil it for 4 or 5 hours in water, ashes and lime
- Carve it into shape
- Forge a stainless steel blade with a single edge
- Emboss the knife with designs or a verse from a *mantinade*
- Find some oleander wood for the sheath. Cut it when the moon is waning or it will soon be oozing worms
- Split the wood in the middle and carve out the interior to fit the blade
- Cut a thin piece of leather into shape and glue it to the sheath
- Fit handle, blade and sheath together, tuck it into your black trousers and look for some *raki*

Cretans take their knives seriously.

Neil Setchfield

Roka Carpets (5, F3)
Watch Manoulis weave his wondrous rugs on a 400-year-old loom using methods that have remained essentially unchanged since Minoan times. Prices begin at 8000 dr for a small rug.
✉ **Zambeliou 61** ☎ **0821-74 736** ⏱ 10am-10pm

Top Hanas Carpet Shop (5, E3)
Specialises in old Cretan kilims (flat-woven rugs) that were traditional dowry gifts; prices start at 30,000 dr.
✉ **Angelou 3** ☎ **0821-58 571** ⏱ 8am-2pm & 5-9pm

FOOD & DRINK
Oinohoos (5, F6)
A fine selection of Greek and Cretan wines, displayed in an appropriately refined shop along with wine implements.
✉ **Sifaka 39** ☎ **0821-27 509** ⏱ **Mon-Fri 8am-1pm & 4-8pm; Sat 8am-1pm**

MUSIC & BOOKS
Georgios Chaicalis Bookshop (5, F4)
Novels, travel guides, translations of Greek classics and maps are on sale here in several languages, including English.
✉ **Plateia Venizelou 12** ☎ **0821-85 236** ⏱ **Mon-Sat 8.30am-1.30pm & 5-9pm**

Studio 2000 (5, H5)
Catering to Cretan tastes for both popular and folk music, this is a good place to pick up a cassette or CD.
✉ **Plateia Agoras 15** ☎ **0821-43 214** ⏱ **Mon-Fri 8am-1pm & 5-8.30pm; Sat 8am-1pm**

IRAKLIO

Iraklio is where the money is, so it's a good place to pick up the latest Cretan fashions, replace a suitcase or shop for luxury goods. **Dedalou** is a pedestrian shopping street lined with some of the classier tourist shops but the market street, **1866**, is a lot more fun. This narrow street is always packed (except on Saturday and Sunday when it is closed) and its stalls spill over with sponges, herbs, fruits, vegetables, utensils, T-shirts, nuts, honey, shoes and jewellery. Look for the ornate Cretan wedding loaves. These round loaves decorated with flower motifs are not meant to be eaten but they do make attractive kitchen decorations. For gold and silver jewellery, head to **Kalokerinou** or the busily commercial **25 Avgoustou**. Kalokerinou is also a good street to buy embroidery, although you'll get better deals in Kritsa. There are no department stores in Iraklio.

CRAFT, ART & ANTIQUES

Octapous (1, C7)
The vast range of merchandise and lengthy opening hours make this a convenient place to browse for T-shirts, cassettes, pottery, postcards, maps, rugs and other souvenirs.
✉ 25 Avgoustou St, No 19 ☎ 081-24 6189 ⏰ 9am-8pm

Spyros Valergos
(1, F6) This is a good stop on colourful 1866 street for ceramics, clothing, statues and icons.
✉ 1866 St, No 5 ☎ 081-28 5019 ⏰ Mon-Fri 8.30am-1pm & 5-8.30pm

LEATHER

Dorcas (1, F7)
The leather handbags, belts, jackets and coats sold here are of high quality, which makes them worth the extra money.
✉ Dedalou 16 ☎ 081-34 6456 ⏰ Mon-Sat 9am-7pm

Tsihlakis (1, F5)
With a mainly local clientele, this shop offers a wide selection of hand-bags and ladies' shoes, some handmade by local artisans.
✉ 1821 St, No 96 ☎ 081-28 2045 ⏰ Mon-Sat 8am-1pm & 4-8pm

MUSIC & BOOKS

Aerakis (1, E7)
This store has a good collection of CDs and cassettes of Cretan and Greek music. Look for the boxed set of *rembetika* by Vassilis Tsitsanis.
✉ Dedalou 35 ☎ 081-225 913 ⏰ Mon-Sat 8am-1pm & 3-7pm

Planet International
(1, D5) This large bookshop has an excellent selection of Greek books translated into English, as well as books on Crete, Greece and a range of Lonely Planet guides.
✉ cnr Hortatson & Kidonias ☎ 081-28 1558 ⏰ Mon, Wed & Sat 8.30am-2.30pm; Tues, Thurs & Fri 8.30am-2pm & 5.30-9pm

Iraklio's upmarket Dedalou St

Neil Setchfield

RETHYMNO

The shopping district of Rethymno is relatively compact, with stores selling everything from souvenirs to jewelled watches. The waterfront promenade of **El Venizelou** has plenty of souvenir shops sandwiched between the restaurants but you'll find higher quality merchandise, including jewellery, on Arkadiou. **Souliou**, a narrow pedestrian street crammed with stores of every kind, makes a wonderful stroll. For fresh produce, don't miss the **Thursday market** (4, J5) on Dimitrikakis.

Worry beads – can I endure another glorious day?

CRAFTS

Katerina Karaoglani
(4, H4) Friendly Katerina makes her pottery in the store. You'll find the standard blue-glazed Cretan ceramics here, but of a better quality than in the tourist shops.
✉ Nikiforou Foka 7
☎ 0831-24 301 ⏰ Mon-Sat 10am-11pm

Melissa (4, H5)
As well as handmade icons, Melissa sells candles, incense, oil lamps and other aromatic items.

✉ Antistaseos 23
☎ 0831-29 601
⏰ Mon-Sat 9am-8pm

Zaharias Theodorakis' workshop (4, F4)
Zaharias turns out onyx bowls and goblets on the lathe at his workshop.
✉ Katehaki 4 ⏰ Mon-Sat 10am-8pm

LEATHER & JEWELLERY

Giorgios Galerakis
(4, G6) The best thing about this jewellery shop, among the many on Arkadiou, is that the ornaments are made on site and you can visit the workshop.
✉ **Arkadiou 201** ☎ 0831-53 704 ⏰ Mon-Sat 9.30am-8pm

Xenia (4, J8)
A Cretan summer makes it hard to think about leather wear, but the suede and leather here is buttery soft and made into elegant ladies' suits, jackets and coats.
✉ **Arkadiou 32 & 265** ☎ 0831-22 045
⏰ Mon-Sat 8.30am-8pm

BOOKS

Ilias Spontidakis
(4, G5) This bookstore is jammed with novels in several languages as well as maps, guidebooks and cassettes of Cretan and Greek music. There's also a small secondhand section.
✉ **Souliou 43** ☎ 0831-54 307 ⏰ Mon-Sat 10am-10pm

International Press Bookshop (4, F6)
As well as foreign newspapers, you'll find a good selection of novels in English, as well as travel guides and history books.
✉ **El Venizelou 81** ☎ 0831-24 111
⏰ Mon-Sat 9am-10pm

Yesterday's cover girls: antique magazine stall

AROUND CRETE

Anogia (2, E8)

Nowhere on Crete is the choice of weavings and embroidery as wide as in Anogia, 37km southwest of Iraklio. Anogia's weaving industry developed after German soldiers in WWII massacred all the townsmen. The surviving women were forced to market their handicrafts and now bring the same sense of desperation to their sales pitches, even though the town has become quite prosperous from cattle breeding. The town is spread out on a hillside with the textile shops in the lower half. Without your own transport you'll face a steep hike to see the upper portion of town.

🚌 5 buses daily from Iraklio (1 hr, 750 dr); Mon-Fri 2 buses daily from Rethymno (1¼ hrs, 1050 dr)

Lappa Avocado

Avocado oil is an excellent treatment for eczema and psoriasis as well as dry skin. The products in this cosy shop are made from high-quality Cretan avocado oil and include face creams, shampoo, soap and sunscreen.

✉ Argiroupolis (2, E5), at the entrance to the old town ☎ 0831-81 264 🚌 Mon-Fri 2 buses daily from Rethymno (40 mins, 460 dr) ⏰ 9.30am-8pm

Margarites (2, E7)

Now that it's on the regular 'Cretan villages' tour itinerary, this potters' village 27km southeast of Rethymno is no longer a provincial backwater. Even if the marketing has got slicker, the pottery is still made the traditional way from local clay. There are numerous stores and workshops, and the neatly turned-out pastel houses make for a pretty stroll. Arrive in the morning or late afternoon, since the town shuts up tight in the afternoon.

🚌 Mon-Fri 2 buses daily from Rethymno

Thrapsano (2, E10)

This quiet town 32km southeast of Iraklio has been turning out clay urns for many centuries. The giant *pithoi* resemble those made by the Minoans and displayed in Knossos but you'll also find more transportable jugs and vases. To see the pithoi makers at work, go downhill to the left of the Plateia to find the workshops. A number of travel agencies throughout the island offer bus tours to Thrapsano but it's easy enough to visit on your own.

🚌 in summer, 4 buses daily from Iraklio (50mins, 400dr)

Union of Agricultural Cooperatives of Sitia

The Sitians are extremely proud of their wine and spirits – and for good reason. The producers have formed a cooperative and offer a free 1hr winery tour that includes a video promoting Sitian wine and olive oil and a wine tasting. The wine is not necessarily cheaper than in the stores but the selection is better and experts are on hand to give advice.

✉ 1km out of Sitia (2, E14) on the road to Agios Nikolaos ☎ 0843-25 200 🚶 walk or taxi from Sitia, or board the bus to/ from Agios Nikolaos ⏰ Mon-Sat 9am-3pm

Thyme-covered hills around Loutro

Diana Mayfield

places to eat

Dining in Crete is refreshingly unpretentious, inexpensive and whole-some. Traditional rural life left women little time to make a fuss over food so they learned to combine fresh local ingredients into hearty, stick-to-the-ribs fare. With its sheep-milk cheeses, wild greens, whole grains, fruits and liberal use of olive oil, the traditional Cretan diet is one of the world's healthiest – though modern life is changing that.

Meal Costs

Dining is relatively inexpensive in Crete no matter where you eat, unless you eat fish. Fresh local fish costs 7500-9000 dr per kilo. The prices in this chapter are based on 2 courses (or a snack in snack places) for 1 person without wine and including cover charge.

$	under 1000 dr
$$	1000-2500 dr
$$$	2500-4000 dr
$$$$	over 4000 dr

Dig in: it's good for you

Local Cuisine

Cretan food and Greek food often overlap. The ubiquitous Greek salad – tomatoes, red peppers, onions, feta cheese and olives – is hard to ruin when the quality of the produce is as high as it is in Crete. *Moussaka*, *pastitsio*, *dolmades* and *yemista* are some of the more popular Greek dishes eaten on Crete.

Cretan and Greek food is served everywhere, but in the major tourist centres menus are also likely to include 'international' dishes such as pizza, schnitzel, spaghetti and hamburgers. These Western dishes are rarely well-executed.

Seafood

The Mediterranean has been seriously over-fished so don't expect any bargains, though you can enjoy tasty sea bream (*skargos*), mullet (*barbounia*) and parrotfish (*skaros*). Fish is usually sold by weight; an average portion is about 300g although in some places the waiter will present you with a tray of fish to make a selection. Regulations require that frozen fish be clearly indicated on the menu although some restaurants try to obscure the information. Shellfish such as shrimp, lobster and calamari are usually frozen.

Meals

Breakfast for Cretans is a powerful little blast of coffee and a pastry. Tourist centres have plenty of places serving overpriced breakfasts but in small villages you'll be lucky to find a *kafeneion* open. Cretans work up an appetite at lunchtime (around 1pm) although you can usually get served earlier. Dinner is late. It's not unusual to see a local taverna swing into action around 11pm after the shops and tourist services close. In the cities, restaurants and tavernas open much earlier for the tourists and many offer service from noon until after midnight.

AGIOS NIKOLAOS

Dining is not the strong point of Agios Nikolaos, possibly because there's not enough of a permanent population to support a thriving restaurant scene. Restaurants that are devoted to soaking up as much money as possible during the tourist season have no incentive to provide consistently good food to a discerning crowd of regulars. **Voulismeni Lake** and the **harbour area** are full of passable but undistinguished restaurants. Most are open until past midnight feeding the night-owls.

Aouas Taverna (3, F2) $$

This is the kind of family-run place where your waiter may be a 10-year-old and the cook is his aunt. The interior is plain but the enclosed garden is refreshing and the *mezedes* are wonderful.

✉ **Paleologou 50** ☎ 0841-23 231 ⏱ noon-midnight ♿ yes **V**

Avli (3, F3) $$

Technically an *ouzeri*, Avli offers an outstanding selection of mezedes. Like many *ouzeria*, it's going upscale and also offers good-value meals in a garden setting.

✉ **Georgiou 12** ☎ 0841-82 479 ⏱ 7pm-midnight ♿ yes **V**

Embassy Garden Restaurant (3, G3) $$

This friendly eatery has a pleasant outdoor terrace and some interesting pasta dishes as well as the standard Cretan fare.

✉ **Kondilaki 5** ☎ 0841-945 57 3915 ⏱ Mar-Nov noon-midnight ♿ yes **V**

New Kow Loon (3, G4) $$

The décor blares 'Chinese', with lots of red, gold and multicoloured lights, the menu is large and the food reasonably authentic. It's a nice change of pace.

Elegant Pelagos: the best eatery in Agios Nikolaos

✉ **Pasifias 1** ☎ 0841-23 891 ⏱ noon-3pm & 6pm-midnight ♿ yes **V**

Pelagos (3, E1) $$$$

For an excellent selection of fresh seafood try Pelagos, generally considered the best restaurant in Agios Nikolaos. Housed in a beautifully restored old house, the elegance extends to fine china and a tranquil garden dining area. Dress code is smart casual and bookings are advisable on weekends.

✉ **Katehaki 10** ☎ 0841-25 737

Non-Boozy Beverages

Water Tap water is purified and safe to drink but most Cretans drink bottled water with their meals. Zaros is a popular brand that comes from a mountain village of the same name (p. 50).

Coffee Eyeball-popping Greek coffee is served in a tiny cup with the grounds and without milk. You can ask for it *glyko* (very sweet), *metrio* (medium sweet) or *sketo* (without sugar). Nescafé is a popular instant coffee served *frappé*, or chilled, in summer.

Tea Not the beverage of choice in Crete, tea is usually available in bags. Herbal tea is becoming popular, especially *diktamos*, or dittany tea.

Fruit Juice Crete produces much more fruit than it can consume or export, which makes fresh squeezed fruit juice relatively good value. Canned fruit juice is also available.

Boozy Beverages

Beer The local beer, Mythos, is cheaper than European brands although both are widely available.

Wine Cretan wine may not make connoisseurs tremble with delight but it can be pleasant and even distinguished. The quality is uneven but the best brands tend to come from Peza, Daphnes, Sitia and Arhanes. The house wine is usually *kokkino*, a cloudy rosé that ranges from drinkable to dreadful. It only costs about 1000 dr a carafe while a good regional wine is at least 3 times as much for a bottle.

Raki Also known as *tsikoudia*, this strong drink made from the residue of grapes is consumed before, during and after meals, and before bed. It's wise to cultivate a taste for the stuff since it's offered everywhere and it's considered impolite to refuse. Although raki is available commercially, Cretan families take pride in producing their own.

Ouzo Another popular spirit made from grape residue, ouzo is flavoured with aniseed. It's drunk straight or mixed with water and usually served with a dish of mezedes.

Retsina A drink that combines wine and pine is not everyone's favourite drop, but once you get past the initial astringency, you may find that this resinated wine is the perfect complement to *tzatziki* and a host of other Cretan dishes.

⏰ Mar-Oct Mon-Sat 7pm-midnight ♿ no **V**

Restaurant du Lac
(3, G3) **$$$**
This busy establishment overlooking Voulismeni Lake is known for its excellent seafood but the menu also boasts a full array of Cretan fare as well as a flashy steak flambé. The restaurant also offers good-value breakfasts and set-price menus. Dress is smart casual.
✉ **Voulismeni Lake** ☎ 0841-22 414 ⏰ mid-Mar to Nov 8am-1am ♿ yes **V**

Sarri's (3, H3) **$**
Not only is Sarri's the best breakfast spot in town, but it stays open until the wee hours serving up mouth-watering food to a neighbourhood crowd. Savouring a souvlaki in the shady courtyard is especially pleasant.
✉ **Kyprou 15** ⏰ 8am-midnight ♿ yes **V**

Taverna Itanos
(3, H3) **$$**
This vast space with beamed ceilings and stucco walls has a few tables on the sidewalk as well as comfortable banquettes. The solid Cretan food is displayed in a glass case and the house wine is more drinkable than most.
✉ **Kiprou 1** ☎ 0841-25 340 ⏰ 9am-11pm ♿ yes **V**

Taverna Pine Tree
(3, F3) **$$**
Dining along scenic Voulismeni Lake is one of the great pleasures of Agios Nikolaos, and this taverna is a good choice. Make your selection from the display case inside and then relax in comfortable wicker chairs and enjoy the view of the lake.
✉ **Paleologou 18** ☎ 0841-23 890 ⏰ 8am-midnight ♿ yes **V**

Ag Nik's waterfront: the perfect setting for al fresco dining

Neil Setchfield

HANIA

Dining along Hania's scenic harbour has an undeniable appeal and the restaurants aren't bad, but the price-quality ratio is low. The best Cretan tavernas are housed in roofless Venetian ruins scattered in the streets of **Splantzia** and the **Old Town**. **Halidon** is a good place to grab a snack.

Adiexodo (5, E3) **$$**
The back-to-basics cuisine here provides a richly satisfying meal. Locals come for the food and the live music on summer nights, packing the tables inside and outside on the narrow pedestrian street.
✉ **Theotokopoulou 59** ☎ **0821-98 882** ⏲ noon-3pm & 7pm-midnight ♿ yes V

Akrogiali **$$$**
Most people consider Akrogiali the best seafood restaurant in Hania. The fish is so fresh it's practically wriggling on the plate, and the accompaniments are superb. The light, airy restaurant opens onto the seafront road, giving you a great view of the sunset.
✉ **Akti Papanikoli 20, Nea Hora** ☎ **0821-71 110** ⏲ Mon-Sat 7pm-midnight ♿ yes V

Anaplous (5, E6) **$$$**
With 4 crumbling walls and no roof, Anaplous has nevertheless achieved a surprising stylishness with a few strategically placed urns and some potted plants. A subdued crowd comes here for traditional Cretan dishes and the occasional guitar player. Come in smart casual attire.
✉ **Sifaka 34** ☎ **0821-41 320** ⏲ 7pm-1am ♿ no V

Apostolis Taverna (5, D7) **$$**
On the quieter eastern harbour, this is a good place for fish and Cretan dishes. Service is friendly and efficient, there's a good wine list and you get a view over the harbour.
✉ **Akti Enoseos 6** ☎ **0821-45 470** ⏲ noon-midnight ♿ yes V

Cafe Eaterie Ekstra (5, F4) **$$**
This friendly, casual eatery is located right in the heart of Hania's bustling Old Town but the cooking is a modern take on traditional Cretan dishes. There are good-value set-price menus and the unusual salads are excellent.
✉ **Zambeliou 8** ☎ **0821-75 725** ⏲ 8am-10pm ♿ yes V

Doloma Restaurant (5, E6) **$$**
This unpretentious restaurant is half-hidden amid the vines and foliage that surround the outdoor terrace. It's a relaxed spot to escape the crowds and the traditional cooking is faultless.
✉ **Kalergon 8** ☎ **0821-51 196** ⏲ Mon-Sat 7.30pm-1am ♿ yes V

Ela (5, G4) **$$**
Dating from the 17th century, the building was first a soap factory, then a school, a distillery and a cheese-processing plant. Now it serves up a well-executed array of Cretan specialities while local musicians create a lively ambience on summer evenings.
✉ **Kondilaki 47** ☎ **0821-74 128** ⏲ noon-1am ♿ yes V

Hippopotamus (5, D7) **$$**
All the usual suspects of Mexican cuisine are present and accounted for in this relaxed hang-out. It attracts an assortment of young, scruffy types who come for the ever-playing Latin music as well as the food.
✉ **Sarpidona 6** ☎ **0821-44 128** ⏲ noon-midnight ♿ yes V

Mezedes

Mezedes are appetisers, served with ouzo at an ouzeria or as the overture to the main meal in tavernas and restaurants. It is perfectly acceptable to make a complete meal out of mezedes, which can be an attractive option for vegetarians. Vegetarian mezedes include *tzatziki, dolmades* and *koukia matsarista* as well as *fasolia* (broad white beans), *saganaki* (fried cheese), *melitzanosalata* (eggplant dip), *tyropitta* (cheese pie) and *spanakopitta* (spinach pie). Meat-eaters can try *bourekaki* (meat pie), *keftedes* (meatballs) and *loukanika* (little sausages).

Kariatis (5, E6) $$

You may hear the strains of Italian opera emanating from Kariatis even before you come to the wide outdoor patio. The Greek dishes are standard but the pizza and pastas are well above average.

✉ Katehaki 12 ☎ 0821-55 600 ◷ noon-3pm & 6pm-midnight ♿ yes V

Katofli $$$

The rustic décor makes a pleasant backdrop for excellent seafood. Katofli is one of 2 outstanding fish restaurants in Hania, located in the city's beach extension, Nea Hora. Try the fish soup (*kakavia*) and wash it down with one of the restaurant's good local wines. Dress smart casual for dinner and book ahead on weekend nights.

✉ Akti Papanikoli 13, Nea Hora ☎ 0821-98 621 ◷ noon-3pm & 7pm-midnight ♿ yes V

Mano Café (5, D3) $

This tiny place has very little seating but offers good-value breakfasts (especially omelets) and snacks if you're in the neighbourhood.

Atmospheric Tamam

✉ Theotokopoulou 62 ◷ 8am-midnight ♿ yes V

Suki Yaki (5, F4) $$

This elaborate Chinese-Thai restaurant offers an intriguing change from Cretan food. The menu is varied and you can eat in the courtyard under an ancient plane tree. There's also an extensive wine list of local and imported wines.

✉ Halidon 28 ☎ 0821-74 264 ◷ noon-midnight ♿ yes V

Tamam (5, F3) $$

Locals find most Old Town restaurants too touristy but Tamam has a loyal following among the trendy set. Housed in the old Turkish baths, this atmospheric place presents a superb array of vegetarian specialities.

✉ Zambeliou 49 ☎ 0821-58 639 ◷ 7.30pm-1am ♿ yes V

Tholos (5, F5) $$$

The building dates from the 14th century and looks it, but the crumbling, roofless walls create a strangely beautiful interior. The fish dishes are good but the speciality here is meat. The restaurant prides itself on its cooked-to-order steaks and tender veal.

✉ Agia Deka 36 ☎ 0821-46 725 ◷ May-Oct noon-midnight ♿ yes V

To Karnagio (5, E6) $$

This is on every Hanian's short-list of favourite restaurants. Its sprawling outdoor terrace near the harbour makes it appealing to tourists but it has not sacrificed one whit of authenticity.

Roofless restaurant

✉ Katehaki 8 ☎ 0821-53 366 ◷ noon-1am ♿ yes V

Tsikoydadiko (5, F4) $$

This restaurant has all the indications of a tourist trap, including a tout outside ready to hook passers-by, and the dreaded 'international' food. Despite all that, the kitchen turns out honest Cretan cooking and the roofless, plant-filled interior is a delight.

✉ Zambeliou 31 ☎ 0821-72 873 ◷ noon-midnight ♿ yes V

Well of the Turk Restaurant & Bar (5, F6) $$$

In the heart of the old Turkish district of Splantzia, this restaurant occupies a former steam bath from the 19th century. Notice the carved relief of Istanbul on the marble fountain. Owned by a British woman, the restaurant features mouth-watering Middle Eastern specialities.

✉ Sarpaki 1 ◷ Wed-Mon 6.30pm-midnight ♿ yes V

Neil Setchfield

IRAKLIO

Iraklio has restaurants to suit all tastes and budgets, from excellent fish tavernas to exotic international cuisine. This businesslike city also has more formal eateries than the rest of the island. Note that the overwhelming majority of restaurants are closed on Sunday. You may have to resort to self-catering, a hotel restaurant or one of the fast-food outlets around the Morosini Fountain.

Aithrion (1, D6) $$$
If you're after a more formal dining experience, head to this upscale restaurant with its full menu of well-prepared Greek specialities. Linen tablecloths and a grand piano set a romantic tone for a meal on the plant-filled terrace. Dress is smart casual and bookings are advisable on weekends, especially late in the evening.
✉ Almyrou & Arholeondos ☎ 081-289 542 ⊘ Mon-Sat 7.30pm-1am ♿ no

Baxes (1, C5) $$
Recently taken over by country folk, this simple restaurant offers Cretan special-occasion cooking. Lamb and goat are stewed for hours or roasted in a brick oven just the way Cretans would cook them for holidays or weddings.
✉ Gianni Chroaki 14 ☎ 081-227 057 ⊘ 11am-2am ♿ yes

Bella Casa (1, G7) $$$
This restaurant is situated in a stunning, turn-of-the-century villa with a small terrace garden on the street. The stylish, pine rooms are air-conditioned in summer, allowing you to savour the richly flavoured Greek and Italian dishes without working up a sweat. Dress smart casual.

✉ Zografou 16 ☎ 081-285 681 ⊘ Mon-Sat noon-5pm & 8pm-1am ♿ no V

Garden of Deykaliola Taverna (1, C4) $$
Wicker chairs, red-checked tablecloths and plastic grapevines put diners in a cheery mood – and that's before the delicious food is served. After the tourists leave at around 11pm, the locals pile in, the owner takes out his accordion and the festivities commence.

Book ahead if you're coming on a weekend night.
✉ Kalokerinou 8 ☎ 081-244 215 ⊘ Mon-Sat 8pm-4am ♿ yes V

Giakoumis (1, F6) $$
Theodosaki is lined with tavernas catering to the market on 1866 and Giakoumis is one of the best. There's a full menu of Cretan specialities and turnover is heavy, which means that the dishes are freshly cooked.

Luscious Mediterranean fare at Loukoulos

Menu Favourites
Boureki Zucchini and cheese in pastry
Dolmades Stuffed vine leaves
Horta Cooked wild greens
Koukia Matsarista Mashed fava beans with potatoes and oil
Moussaka Layers of eggplant, minced meat and potatoes topped with sauce and baked
Pastitsio Baked, cheese-topped macaroni and meat
Stifado Meat stew made from beef, goat or rabbit
Tzatziki Yoghurt with cucumber and garlic
Yemista Stuffed tomatoes or green capsicums

✉ Theodosaki 5-8
🕐 Mon-Sat noon-3pm
& 7-10pm ♿ yes **V**

Giovanni Taverna
(1, E7) **$$$$**
This is a splendid place, with 2 floors of large, airy rooms and, in summer, outdoor eating on a quiet pedestrian street. The food is a winning Mediterranean combination of Greek and Italian specialities, prepared with care and imagination. Dress smart and book ahead for dinner on weekends.
✉ Korai 12 ☎ 0831-346 338 🕐 Mon-Sat noon-2.30pm & 7.30pm-midnight ♿ yes **V**

Ippokampos Ouzeri
(1, B6) **$$**
This is as good as taverna-style eating gets. The interior is attractively decorated with cooking pots but most people try to squeeze in at one of the sidewalk tables. Whether you opt for vegetarian mezedes or baked squid, you'll find the food fresh and savoury. As proof of its quality, the taverna is always packed.
✉ Mitsotaki 2 ☎ 081-280 240 🕐 Mon-Fri noon-3pm & 7.30pm-midnight; Sat noon-3pm ♿ yes **V**

Katsina Ouzeri
(1, C6) **$$**
This is an old neighbourhood favourite. Most people come for the lamb and pork roasted in a brick oven, or the excellent stewed goat. Portions are hearty and the atmosphere is convivial.
✉ Marineli 12 🕐 Tues-Sun 7pm-1am ♿ yes **V**

Loukoulos
(1, E7) **$$$$**
Dine on luscious Mediterranean specialities served on fine china and accompanied by soft classical music. You can eat either in the elegant interior or on the outdoor terrace under a lemon tree. All the vegetables are organically grown and vegetarians are well cared for. Dress is smart casual.
✉ Korai 5 ☎ 081-224 435 🕐 Mon-Sat noon-3pm & 7pm-midnight ♿ no **V**

Loukoumades
(1, E6) **$**
Loukoumades are honey-dipped fritters and this hole-in-the-wall near the Morosini fountain has the best in town. Workers, shopkeepers and businesspeople drift in and out all day for their loukoumades fix but, on a scale of 1 to 10, the ambience is minus 6.
✉ Dikeosynis 8

Dining Establishments

Kafeneia These coffee-houses are open from morning to night (sometimes with an afternoon break) for a clientele consisting almost exclusively of older Cretan men playing cards or backgammon. They don't serve food but the drinks are fairly cheap.

Ouzeria Traditionally places to drink ouzo and nibble mezedes, ouzeria are going upscale and sometimes offer menus with a large choice of appetisers and daily specials.

Zaharoplasteia When a Cretan is hit by a sugar craving, they'll head to a zaharoplasteia for a gooey pastry, chocolate or honey-dipped sweet. Drinks are also available and sometimes there's seating.

Taverna The traditional Cretan taverna is an informal establishment of plastic tablecloths, paper napkins and freshly cooked local dishes. You're expected to peer into the pots of food in the back and nod appreciatively before making your selection.

Estiatoria Although the line between the 2 is blurring, restaurants tend to be more formal and expensive than tavernas. The food, though, is not necessarily any better. As in tavernas, you can often inspect the daily offerings in the back before sitting down to eat.

Pull up a chair and grab an ouzo at an ouzeri

Neil Setchfield

☎ 081-346 005 ⏱
5am-midnight ♿ yes

New China (1, E7) **$$**
Every truly cosmopolitan
city has a Chinese restau-
rant, and Iraklio is no
exception. There's an
extensive menu of compe-
tent Chinese dishes –
slightly adapted to please
local palates – and a
pleasant courtyard.
✉ **Korai 1** ☎ 081-245
162 ⏱ Mon-Sat noon-
3pm & 7pm-midnight ♿
yes **V**

Restaurant Ionia
(1, F6)   **$$**
This is the place for good,
down-home Cretan cook-
ing. Make your choice from
the pots and pans of food
on display, sit down and
enjoy a scrumptious meal.
✉ **cnr Evans & Giannari**
⏱ Mon-Sat 7pm-mid-
night ♿ yes **V**

Ta Leontaria 1922
(1, E6)   **$**
The delicious cheese-filled
bougatsa served here has
a loyal following among
Iraklio's older set, who linger
for hours over bougatsa,
coffee and water, watching
the crowds mill around the
Morosini fountain.
✉ **facing the Morosini
fountain** ⏱ 7am-
midnight ♿ yes **V**

Taverna Kastella
(1, B5)   **$$**
The food here is good but
the setting is better. The
taverna is right on the
water, offering a spectacu-
lar view of the Venetian
fortress. Come at the end
of the day and enjoy the
sunset over an ouzo and
mezedes.
✉ **S Venizelou 3** ☎
081-284 432 ⏱ Mar-

Dining Customs

Dining is a casual affair in Crete. In traditional taver-
nas, food is served all at once, often lukewarm and
doused with lots of olive oil, which is the way
Cretans like it. If you're dining in a group, the waiter
will place your orders in the centre of the table so the
dishes can be shared. Food is often eaten with the
fingers. Although you'll see some fixed-price menus
in tourist restaurants, most Cretans prefer to sample
an assortment of dishes rather than confine them-
selves to an appetiser, main course and dessert.
Often the meal ends with a complimentary shot of
raki and a dish of seasonal fruit.

A cover charge of 150-300 dr is tacked onto the
bill. A service charge is included although it's custom-
ary to leave a few hundred drachma in appreciation.

Street-side tables let you enjoy the sun and the food.

Nov 9.30-12.30am ♿
yes **V**

Tierra del Fuego
(1, C5)   **$$$**
Mexican food is trendy
right now in Crete, making
Tierra del Fuego popular
with a hip, young crowd.
You'll need to book ahead
for late dinners on week-
ends. If you're not hell-bent
on authenticity, you'll be
amused by the Cretan ver-
sions of Mexican standards.
✉ **Theotokopoulou 26**
☎ 081-289 542 ⏱
Mon-Sat 8pm-midnight
♿ no

Vareladika Ouzeri
(1, C6)   **$$**
This cheerful place has been
taken over by a Greek-
American couple who have
spruced up the interior
while maintaining the
ouzeri's tradition of serving

simple, well-prepared
Cretan dishes. Try the excel-
lent sea-urchin salad.
✉ **Moni Agarathou 13**
☎ 081-222 505
⏱ Mon-Sat noon-
2.30pm & 7pm-mid-
night ♿ yes **V**

*Giovanni: a winning
Greek-Italian combination*

RETHYMNO

The waterfront along **El Venizelou** is lined with mirror-image tourist restaurants staffed by fast-talking waiters desperately cajoling passers-by into their establishments. The situation is much the same around the **Venetian harbour**, except that the setting is better and the prices higher. The most authentic places are in the web of side streets inland from the harbour.

Dining on Rethymno harbour

Avli (4, F5) $$$$
There's no better place in town than Avli for a romantic evening out. The food is superb and this former Venetian villa has an idyllic enclosed garden for dining al fresco. Dress smart casual.
✉ **Xanthoudidou 22**

Stella's Kitchen

☎ 0831-26 213 ☺ noon-2.30pm & 6pm-midnight ♿ yes **V**

Famagousta (4, E5) $$$
This local favourite has a large menu of Greek and international dishes but the best choices are the Cypriot specialities. Try the delicious lamb cooked in a clay oven or the meatballs with yoghurt and pita.
✉ **Plastira 6** ☎ 0831-23 881 ☺ noon-3pm & 7pm-midnight ♿ yes **V**

Fanari (4, J1) $$
Tourists rarely wander this far west, but this is as typical a taverna as you're likely to find in Rethymno. The fish is fresh, carnivores will love the grilled steak and the homemade wine is surprisingly good.
✉ **Kefalogiani 15** ☎ 0831-54 849 ☺ noon-midnight ♿ yes **V**

Gounakis Restaurant & Bar (4, G3) $$
This fun place is worth visiting for its food as much as for its music. The plain interior contains a small stage at the back that attracts some of Rethymno's finest folk musicians. The cooking is delicious.
✉ **Koroneou 6** ☎ 0831-28 816 ☺ 8pm-1am ♿ yes **V**

Old Town Taverna (4, G4) $$$
This is a good spot to come after exploring the Historical & Folk Art Museum right across the street. The traditional Cretan food is well prepared and there's a good-value set-price menu with wine.
✉ **Vernardou 31** ☎ 0831-26 436 ☺ noon-3pm & 7pm-midnight ♿ yes **V**

O Psaras (4, F4) $$$
The fish at this unpretentious taverna is always fresh, making it popular with locals and visitors alike. The tables are outside on an attractive square next to a church.
✉ **Arabatzoglou 69** ☎ 0831-22 738 ☺ noon-midnight ♿ yes **V**

Stella's Kitchen (4, G5) $
This tiny, homey spot on one of Rethymno's oldest streets serves up tasty snacks and a few meals.

It's a good bet for breakfast as well. There are only a couple of tables, so you may have to take the food away.

✉ **Souliou 55** ⏰ **8am-midnight** ♿ **yes**

Sunset (4, E1) $$

Let the tourists eat elbow-to-elbow on Venizelou street. Sunset is on the other side of the Venetian fortress where all is calm. You can feast on decent Cretan dishes while seated right along the water. Come at sunset, of course.

✉ **Periferiakos, beneath the fortress** ☎ **0831-23 943** ⏰ **noon-midnight** ♿ **yes** Ⓥ

Taverna Kastro (4, F3) $$

This out-of-the-way restaurant often has space when others are full. The enclosed garden terrace provides a soothing setting for decent Cretan dishes.

✉ **Melissinou 17** ☎ **0831-22 666** ⏰ **noon-midnight** ♿ **yes** Ⓥ

Taverna Kyria Maria (4, F5) $$

For authentic atmosphere, wander inland down the little side streets to Kyria Maria, behind the Rimondi fountain. This cosy, traditional taverna has outdoor seating under a leafy trellis with twittering birds. All meals end with a complimentary dessert and shot of raki.

✉ **Fotaki 22** ☎ **0831-29 078** ⏰ **8am-1am** ♿ **yes** Ⓥ

Taverna Pontios (4, F4) $$

Taverna Pontios is proof that some of the best Cretan food comes from places that look like upgraded street stalls. A convivial group of locals descend on Pontios for the delicious cheese-stuffed calamari, among other dishes.

✉ **Melissinou 34** ⏰ **noon-2.30pm & 6pm-midnight** ♿ **yes** Ⓥ

Taverna Zisis $$$

When Rethymno couples and their kids, grandparents, cousins, aunts and nephews want to make a night of it, they'll head to the vast Taverna Zisis. Vegetarians beware: nearly all the dishes involve meat, whether broiled, grilled, stewed or fried.

✉ **Mahis Kritis 17, Missiria (2, E6), 2km east of Rethymno on the coast road** ☎ **0831-28 814** ⏰ **noon-3pm & 6pm-midnight** ♿ **yes**

The Good Oil

If you want to irritate a Cretan, praise Italian olive oil. So many olives, so much olive oil, and most goes to Italy to be repackaged under Italian brand names. Despite the rich, fruity flavour of Cretan olive oil, it has lost out in the global sweepstakes to Italy's formidable distribution network. Cretans are assiduously promoting their oil in international contests and fairs but it remains a rarity on most supermarket shelves.

Harvest season begins in November and ends in February. Although harvesting machines are used in some places, olives are mostly collected by raking or shaking the tree branches until the olives fall into nets. Sacks of olives are taken to olive presses that extract the oil either by centrifugal force or by crushing them in moving millstones. The oil is filtered and separated from the water before being stored in steel basins. Bottling is fully automated.

Stock up – and don't mention the Italian stuff

Neil Setchfield

AROUND CRETE

If you're travelling around Crete, you're sure to find a good feed at the establishments listed below. Cretan menus are more or less the same around the island, with few regional variations, but if you're in the Sfakia region be sure to sample one of the famous Sfakian cheese pies served in most local tavernas. The Balcony in Sitia is worth a detour for its outstanding and unusual dishes.

WEST

Grammeno $$

Few tourists make it to the town of Grammeno, which leaves this exceptional taverna to the locals. Among the Cretan specialities on offer are a delicious rabbit stewed in *mizithra* (sheep's-milk cheese) and stuffed zucchini flowers.

✉ Grammeno, 5km west of Paleohora (2, F2) ☎ 0823-41 505 🚌 head west out of Paleohora along the coast road and you'll see the restaurant on the right ⏰ Apr-Oct 7pm-1am ♿ yes V

Mylos $$$

The food is good but it's worth dining here for the setting alone. The centrepiece of the restaurant is an old flour-mill beside a pool loaded with geese. The surrounding dining rooms are lush with flowers, trees and vines. Dress is smart casual.

✉ main road in Platanias (2, D2) ☎ 0821-68 578 🚌 buses between Hania and Kastelli-Kissamos stop in Platanias ⏰ Mar-Nov 7pm-midnight; weekends only in winter ♿ yes V

The Third Eye $$

The Third Eye has one of the more unusual menus on the island, with an assortment of Asian-inspired dishes and a range of curry sauces. It's always busy, so come early.

✉ around the corner from the Pal Beach hotel, Paleohora (2, F2) ☎ 0823-41 234 ⏰ Apr-Oct 7pm-midnight ♿ yes V

CENTRAL

Kombos $$$

When locals from Rethymno are looking for a special meal, they'll pile into cars and drive to Atsipopoulo. On the edge of the village, this friendly taverna specialises in meaty meals. The lamb is good and, if you're up to it, try the *splinogardouba* (spleen).

✉ Atsipopoulo (2, E6), 3km southwest of Rethymno ☎ 0831-29 725 🚌 head west out of Rethymno and turn south on the road to Episkopi; you'll see the restaurant before entering the village ⏰ 7pm-1am ♿ yes

Mihalis $$$

This village taverna is outstanding both in the quality of the cuisine and the authentically Cretan ambience. It really gets going after midnight when Mihalis might bring out his guitar for a set of traditional Cretan tunes.

✉ Roumeli (2, D7), 24km east of Rethymno ☎ 0834-51 264 🚌 go east from Rethymno along the coastal road to Iraklio. At the Panormos junction, turn right following the signs to Perama (2, D7). Turn left after the bridge and follow the signs to Roumeli. Mihalis is the only taverna in town. ⏰ 7pm-1am ♿ yes V

Mystical View Restaurant $$

Perched on a cliff overlooking the Messara Gulf, this restaurant has views that live up to its name, and it serves good food to boot.

✉ 3km northeast of Matala (2, F7) ☎ 0892-094 139 164 🚌 from Matala, take the road to Phaestos and follow the signs to the restaurant ⏰ noon-midnight ♿ yes V

Taverna Diktina $$

In a dreamy setting along the beach, this special taverna emphasises vegetarian food, with giant salads, fresh fish and refreshing fruit drinks.

✉ beach road, Arvi (2, F11) ☎ 0895-71 249 🚌 from Iraklio follow the main road southeast to Ano Viannos; about 8km past the town you'll see the turn-off for Arvi ⏰ noon-midnight ♿ yes V

Taverna Nikitas $$

This simple taverna is right on the sea but specialises in roast lamb and pork, although there is usually a good selection of fresh fish. ✉ **Keratokambos (2, F11), 70km southeast of Iraklio** 🚌 **follow the main road southeast to Ano Viannos and take the Keratokambos turn-off 3km before the town** ☎ **0895-51 477** ⏰ **8am-midnight** ♿ **yes** **V**

Taverna Stratidakis $$

Madam Stratidakis moves slowly but she's a demon in the kitchen. Whatever daily specials are bubbling away in the back, you can be sure of having a memorable meal in this simple taverna. ✉ **main road, Spili (2, E6)** ☎ **0832-22 006** 🚌 **Spili is on the Rethymno-Agia Galini bus route with 4 buses daily** ⏰ **8am-midnight** ♿ **yes** **V**

Votomos $$

Trout is the speciality at this superb seafood restaurant affiliated with the Hotel Idi (p. 105). You'll see the trout gliding through a huge freshwater reserve so you'll know they're fresh. The fresh mountain air will whet your appetite. ✉ **Zaros (2, F8), 42km southwest of Iraklio** ☎ **0894-31 666** ⏰ **Mar-Oct 11am-midnight; weekends only in winter** ♿ **yes** **V**

EAST

Napoleon $$

Napoleon bills itself as the oldest restaurant in Ierapetra and it maintains a traditional aura. The Greek/Cretan specialities are cooked to perfection and the restaurant has a lovely setting along the water. ✉ **Samouil 10, Ierapetra (2, F12)** ⏰ **noon-midnight** ♿ **yes** **V**

Steki $$

This is a traditional taverna where ceiling fans twirl overhead, Greek music plays in the background and you're invited to examine the pots of freshly prepared food. There's an excellent selection of mezedes. ✉ **Papandreou 13, Sitia (2, E14)** ☎ **0843-22 857** ⏰ **8am-midnight** ♿ **yes** **V**

A new dimension: The Balcony in Sitia

Neil Setchfield

The Balcony $$$$

'Discover a new dimension in the Greek food you already know and love' proclaims the brochure for The Balcony, and it is entirely correct. Opened by a former actor, this restaurant takes an extraordinarily imaginative approach to Greek cuisine, borrowing ideas from Mexican, Italian and Asian dishes. It also has air-con. ✉ **Kazantzaki & Foundalidou, Sitia (2, E14)** ☎ **0843-25 084** ⏰ **noon-3pm & 7pm-midnight** ♿ **yes** **V**

INTERNET CAFES

Istos Cyber Cafe

This small cyber cafe has a fast connection, several computers and also offers scanning, printing and faxing services. ✉ **Malikouti 2, Iraklio** ☎ **081-22 2120** ⏰ **9am-1am**

Net c@fe

There are only a couple of computers and a few soft drinks but the connection is good and there are printing facilities. ✉ **Venieri 2, Rethymno** ☎ **0832-55 133** ⏰ **10am-10pm**

Polychoros

This cyber cafe overlooking Lake Voulismeni is a nice place to hang out even if you don't need to use the computers. There's a great selection of Greek CDs. ✉ **28 Oktovriou, Agios**

Nikolaos (3, G3)   ☎

0841-24 876 @ **peripou @agn.forthnet.gr** ⏰ **9am-2am**

Vranas Studios

This spacious and comfortable cyber cafe has 5 computers and printing facilities. ✉ **Ag Deka and Sarpaki, Hania** ☎ **0821-58 618** @ **vranas@yahoo. com** ⏰ **8am-midnight**

entertainment

Entertainment in Crete ranges from the touristy to the traditional. Coastal towns naturally cater to international visitors, with outdoor discos and beachside bars blaring Western rock music. The further inland you go, the more you are likely to encounter traditional music and dancing, especially at village tavernas. High-brow European culture has never caught on in Crete, perhaps because local music and dancing are so complex and interesting. Very few international ballet troupes, orchestras and opera companies come to Crete. If they do, their visit most likely coincides with the Iraklio Summer Festival (see What's On opposite). The festival also stages ancient Greek dramas, which are the highlight of the Cretan theatrical year.

Cinema

Like Greeks in general, Cretans are keen movie-goers. Almost every town of consequence has a cinema. English-language films are shown in English with Greek subtitles. Admission ranges from 1000 dr in small-town movie houses to 1800 dr at plush big-city cinemas.

Nightlife

Discos are dotted around big cities and resort areas, though not in the numbers of a decade ago. Most young Cretans prefer to head for the music bars that have proliferated to fill the void. These bars normally specialise in a particular style of music - Greek, modern rock, 60s rock, techno and, very occasionally, jazz. Western rock music continues to grow in popularity but live music remains a rarity.

Traditional Music & Dancing

Cretans are proud of their rich tradition of folk songs and dances. In village tavernas late at night someone is bound to produce a lyra and inspire a group sing-along. Weddings are great opportunities to catch a glimpse of authentic local culture.

Cretan music is often played in restaurants and clubs during the tourist season although it's usually altered to appeal to tourists.

Folk dancing is an integral part of all festival celebrations and there is often impromptu folk dancing in tavernas.

If you're in Crete in summer, you may miss the pre-eminent Cretan folk dancers, many of whom go on tour in summer. If you're in Athens, you can see Cretan dancers perform nightly in summer at the Dora Stratou Theatre. Another Cretan group, the Nelly Dimoglou Dance Company, performs at the Old City Theatre in Rhodes City.

Cretan Music

Cretan music, woven tightly into the fabric of everyday life, accompanies weddings, births, deaths, holidays, harvesting and simply relaxing. The main instruments are the *lyra*, which is similar to a violin, and the 8-stringed *lute*, which is played like a guitar. Traditional Cretan songs include *mantinades*, improvised couplets that express the age-old concerns of love, death and the vagaries of fate, and *rizitika* which are centuries-old songs from the Lefka Ori.

What's On

March-April *Easter* – for more information see page 96

April *Feast Day of St George (Agios Georgios)* – 23 Apr; the patron saint of shepherds is most elaborately celebrated in Asi Gonias, where thousands of goats and sheep are gathered at the town church for shearing, milking and blessing and locals drink fresh milk and feast

May *Battle of Crete* – last week; the town of Hania commemorates this costly WWII battle with athletic competitions, folk dancing and ceremonial events

June *Marine Week* – last week, even numbered years; Crete's harbour cities stage music and dance events on land, and swimming and sailing competitions on the water

July *Wine Festival of Rethymno* – held in the municipal park, the festival offers wine-tasting and local cuisine for an admission of about 1000 dr

July-August *Renaissance Festival* – Rethymno's main cultural event features dance, drama and films as well as art exhibitions

Krvia Festival – Ierapetra stages various musical, theatrical and artistic presentations

Kornaria Festival – Sitia puts on music and theatre events, as well as art exhibits, races and a beach volleyball competition

Iraklio Summer Arts Festival – international artists as well as local singers and dancers perform at the Nikos Kazantzakis Open Air Theatre (p. 94)

Lato Festival – Agios Nikolaos hosts traditional and modern works performed by local and international orchestras and dance troupes

August *Paleohora Music Festival* – 1-10 Aug; the town is devoted to music for 10 days, with song contests and concerts staged every night

Cultural Festival – 3-day festival in Ano Viannos which features concerts, plays and art exhibits

Feast of the Assumption – 15 Aug; an important religious holiday – in the town of Arhanes, the day is the conclusion of a 5-day wine festival celebrating the excellent local wine

Sultana Festival – last week of August; Sitia celebrates its superior sultana raisins with wine, music and dancing

Potato Festival – the Lassithi region produces superior potatoes, which is cause enough for a 3-day celebration in Tzermiado

Traditional Cretan Wedding – Kritsa stages a traditional Cretan wedding replete with songs, dancing and traditional food

October *Chesnut Festival* – 3rd Sunday; the village of Elos offers everyone roasted chestnuts, chestnut sweets and tsikoudia

'No' Day – 28 Oct; commemorates Prime Minister Metaxas' `no' to Mussolini's ultimatum of 1940, it is celebrated with parades, dances and feasts

November *Arkadiou Monastery Anniversary* – 7-9 Nov; anniversary of the explosion in 1866 which claimed almost 1000 Cretan lives, this tragic event is commemorated at the monastery (p. 48) and is one of Crete's most important holidays

AGIOS NIKOLAOS

You don't need a guide to find the nightlife in Agios Nikolaos; the nightlife will find you. This is a town that slumbers during the day and comes alive at night. As soon as the heat of the day passes, the cafes and bars along the harbour open one by one and by midnight the action is in full swing. Just head to the streets around the **harbour** and look for a place that appeals.

Catch the latest flicks at Rex

Neil Setchfield

Cafe du Lac (3, G3)
Cafe du Lac is a quiet place to take a breather from the frenzied harbour nightlife. It has modern décor and a soothing view over Voulismeni Lake.
✉ **28 Octovriou** ☎ **0841-26 837** ⏰ **10am-midnight**

Enplo (3, F4)
On a bluff overlooking the harbour, Enplo is a subdued bar/cafe, usually less crowded than the bars below. The music is '80s and '90s rock.
✉ **Akti Koundourou 4** ☎ **0841-25 831** ⏰ **Mar-Nov 10am-midnight**

Lipstick Disco (3, F4)
It's loud, crowded and overpriced but Lipstick is Agios Nikolaos' premier disco. In fact, it's the only disco. You'll see many foreigners but very few locals.
✉ **Akti Koundourou** ⏰ **Apr-Oct 11pm-dawn**

Rex 'Polycenter' (3, G4)
This 300-seat convention centre is also a cinema presenting first-run movies.
✉ **M Sfakianaki** ☎ **0841-83 681**

Rififi (3, G3)
Along the lively Agios Nikolaos harbour, Rififi provides a raucous good time to a late-night crowd.
✉ **25 Martiou** ☎ **0841-23 140** ⏰ **Apr-Oct 10pm-dawn**

Royale Bar (3, G3)
A perennial favourite, the Royale Bar is known for its excellent cocktails and relentlessly upbeat mood. It's no place for quiet conversation but a good place to meet people.
✉ **25 Martiou** ☎ **0841-26 476** ⏰ **6pm-2am**

Santa Maria (3, G3)
The Santa Maria bar provides a more local ambience than many other bars along the waterfront. There's no live music but the bar has a good selection of contemporary Greek popular music on disc.
✉ **M Sfakianaki** ☎ **0841-22 984** ⏰ **Apr-Oct 10pm-2am**

HANIA

Funky rock & roll joints play the dominant role in Hania's nightlife but there are also some cosy spots for jazz, light rock and Cretan music. When Hanians want to party the night away at a disco, they'll likely head out to **Platanias**, a coastal resort about 11km west of town.

Angeli Café (5, E3)
On the waterfront, this joint plays rock music at a volume that renders conversation possible only for lip readers. But you can escape to the outdoor terrace.
✉ **Kountourioti 54** ☎ **0821-74 960** ☽ 8am-1am

Ariadne (5, E5)
Formerly a disco, Ariadne has taken on a sleek new look and now uses its excellent sound system to play a variety of music. Usually there's jazz early in the evening and rock later on. There's a wide range of drinks on offer and some *mezedes*.
✉ **Akti Tobazi 2** ☎ **0821-50 987** ☽ 10am-1am

Café Crete (5, E7)
Café Crete is a rough-and-ready joint with a decorative scheme that relies on saws, pots, old sewing machines and animal heads. It's also the best place in Hania to hear live Cretan music. If they don't bring their own *lyra*, locals will reach for the instruments that line the walls once they've had a couple of drinks. Beware the *kamakia* (see at right).
✉ **Kalergon 22** ☎ **0821-58 661** ☽ 6pm-1am

Dyo Lux (5, E8)
If Che Guevara was alive and in Hania, he'd feel at

Background reading at Fortezza

Neil Setchfield

home in this 'alternative cafe'. The music is Latin American, reading material of a countercultural nature is strewn about, and the cosy seating is perfect for plotting revolutions.
✉ **Sarpidona 8** ☎ **0821-52 515** ☽ 10am-midnight

Fagotto Jazz Bar (5, E3)
Black & white photographs of jazz greats line the walls of this bar,

housed in a restored Venetian building and offering the smooth sounds of jazz and light rock. Sometimes in summer there's a live jazz group.
✉ **Angelou 16** ☎ **0821-71 887** ☽ 7pm-2am

Fortezza (5, C7)
This cafe/bar/restaurant installed in the old Venetian ramparts is the best place in town for a

Kamakia

The word means 'fishing tridents' and is applied to Greek men who 'fish' for foreign women in order to have a sexual encounter that they can brag about to their friends. (There's no word for the reverse situation which is probably as common.) These guys are usually found trawling the tourist bars with the same bait their dads used: 'Where are you from? You are beautiful. May I buy you a drink?'. They're not hard to get rid of. A firm 'aee hasou' (get away!) usually does the trick. After all, there are plenty of fish in the sea.

sunset drink. A free barge takes you across the water from the bottom of Sarpidona street to the sea wall wrapping around the harbour. From the rooftop bar, there's a splendid view of the Venetian harbour.
✉ **Old Harbour** ☎ **0821-46 546** ☼ **Apr-Oct 10am-1am**

Four Seasons (5, D6)
This rock bar on the harbour attracts a fashionable group of young Hanians. The harbourside terrace is always full and the atmosphere is friendly.
✉ **Akti Tobazi 29** ☎ **0821-55 583** ☼ **10am-1am**

Ideon Antron (5, F4)
In the middle of busy, touristy Halidon street, this place offers a more sophisticated atmosphere with discreet music and garden seating.
✉ **Halidon 26** ☎

0821-95598 ☼ **noon-midnight**

Point Music Bar
(5, E5) This is a good rock bar for those allergic to techno and house. When the interior gets steamy you can cool off on the 1st-floor balcony overlooking the harbour.
✉ **Sourmeli 2** ☎ **0821-57 556** ☼ **9.30pm-2am**

Rudi's Bierhaus
(5, E6) Austrian Rudi Riegler packs this tiny bar with fine Belgian *guezes* and *krieks* as well as other excellent beers. He also serves some of the best mezedes in town.
✉ **Sifaka 26** ☼ **Mon-Sat 6pm-midnight**

Street Club (5, E3)
The cave-like interior of this harbourside club is filled with the sounds of soul and Latin music. On Sunday at noon a guest DJ

arrives to play the latest tracks.
✉ **Akti Kountourioti 51** ☎ **0821-74 960** ☼ **11am-1am**

Synagogi (5, F4)
Housed in a roofless Venetian building that was once a synagogue, Synagogi serves up fresh fruit juices, coffee, drinks and snacks. The stone and wood interior is stunning and there's a good selection of rock music playing in the background.
✉ **Skoufon 15** ☎ **0821-96 797**

The Game (5, G4)
Take the first narrow passage on Halidon next to the Hania Exchange bank and you'll come to Hania's main disco. The crowd is aged 18-21 and the music is deep house and techno.
✉ **off Halidon** ☎ **0821-72 768** ☼ **midnight-5am**

Soul and Latin sounds fill the cave-like interior of the Street Club.

Neil Setchfield

IRAKLIO

Nightlife in Iraklio offers an incredible range of experiences, from soft music and herbal tea to pounding discos. There are 5 major nightlife neighbourhoods, each with its own style. The bars and cafes around **Plateia Venizelou** are as hyped-up as the non-stop crowds milling around the Morosini fountain. The pedestrian area of **Korai** and **Perdikari** is lined with stylish *kafeneia* that attract a before-disco crowd eager to see and be seen. The old buildings along **Handakos St** contain relaxed bar/cafes with cosy interiors and enclosed patios more suited to conversation than people-watching. **Dukos Beaufort** street, under the Archaeological Museum, has several sleek, well-behaved discos, while the venues on **Ikarou Avenue** (p. 94) have a rougher edge.

The **Iraklio Summer Arts Festival** presents international guest orchestras and dance troupes as well as local talent. Concerts and stage productions are offered sporadically the rest of the year; the tourist office of Iraklio will have the latest schedules.

Aktapika (1, E6)
This large airy space next to the Morosini fountain is bustling day and night. It's a good place to come early in the evening for people-watching.
✉ Dedalou 2 ☎ 081-341 225 ⏱ 10am-1am

Astoria Cinema
(1, F8) Conveniently located in the town centre, the Astoria shows first-run movies in their original language – usually English.
✉ Plateia Eleftherias ☎ 081-226 191 ⏱ Sept-April

De Facto (1, E6)
Although busy all day, De Facto is one of the most fashionable bars in town early in the evening when it offers ringside seats to the evening promenade around Morosini fountain. It's also very gay-friendly.
✉ Kantanoleon 21 ☎ 081-342 007 ⏱ noon-midnight

Four Lions (1, E6)
The restaurant is down-stairs but the rooftop bar is a great perch for watching the goings-on around the Morosini fountain, directly below. A subdued crowd chats in comfortable chairs around a replica of the famous Four Lions fountain.
✉ Plateia Venizelou ☎ 081-280 732 ⏱ noon-midnight

Guernica (1, D4)
Traditional décor and contemporary rock in one of Iraklio's hippest bar/cafes. The terrace-garden of this rambling old building is a delight in summer, and in winter you can warm up next to the fireplace.
✉ A Kritis 2 ☎ 081-282 988 ⏱ 10am-midnight

The Ice Factory/ Pagopeion (1, D7)
This former ice factory is the most original bar/restaurant on the island. There's almost too much to look at in its whimsical space but don't miss the surrealistic toilets. The restaurant serves dishes with names like 'Roll With Me, Baby' pasta and 'Arm Agadon' peppers. A DJ comes at around 10pm to spin jazz, rock and techno and the ambience is gay-friendly.
✉ Plateia Agios Titos ☎ 081-346 028 ✉ www.members.tripod.com/~icefactory ⏱ 8am-midnight

Ideon Antron (1, E7)
On trendy Korai street, with its rows of postmodern kafeneia, Ideon Antron is a throwback. The stone interior with its shiny wood bar creates a relaxed, inviting space.
✉ Perdikari 1, corner of Korai ☎ 081-242 041 ⏱ 10am-1am

Jasmin (1, C4)
This friendly bar/cafe with a back terrace specialises in herbal tea but also serves alcohol. The nightly DJs play rock and world music as well as techno.
✉ Handakos 45 ☎ 081-288 880 ⏱ noon-midnight

Nikos Kazantzakis Open Air Theatre
(1, K6) This immense open-air theatre is the main venue for Iraklio's Summer Arts Festival when musicians, actors and dancers perform under the stars. It's also used as an open-air cinema in summer, and special events take place the rest of the year.
✉ **Jesus Bastion** ☎ 081-242 977 ⏰ box office 9am-2.30pm & 6.30-9.30pm

The Ikarou Group

You may not want to buy real estate on Ikarou Avenue, but this action-packed street serves up the wildest nightlife in town. The following venues open around midnight, close near dawn and devote the intervening hours to keeping a young crowd of clubbers in perpetual motion. The music is a contemporary mix of rock, techno and Greek. One or more of these venues is likely to be closed weeknights in summer when the club scene moves to Ammoudara.

At No 11 there's **DNA** (1, E9; ☎ 081-221 206) and **Politia** (☎ 081-222 241); **Fougaro** (1, F9; ☎ 081-330 069), **Kratitirio** (☎ 081-229 850) and **Vareladiko** are at No 9 and **Silo Club** (☎ 081-244 949) is at No 24. Wear black.

DNA serves up a wild mix of rock, techno and Greek.

Privilege Club
(1, D10) Iraklio's smart set packs this recently refurbished dance club that easily holds 1000 people. Like many of Crete's dance clubs, there's international music (rock, techno etc) until about 2am, when Greek music takes over. Wear smart casual.
✉ **Dukos Beaufort 7** ☎ 081-343 500 ⏰ 11pm-dawn

Sousouro (1, E6)
Sit outside and watch the scene around Korai or retreat to the artsy interior where a pianist entertains most evenings.
✉ **Androgeo 9** ☎ 081-226 510 ⏰ 6pm-1am

Take Five (1, D6)
This old favourite on the edge of El Greco park gets going after sundown, when the outside tables fill up with a diverse crowd of regulars, including many gays. The music and ambience are low-key.
✉ **Arkoleontos 7** ☎ 081-226 564 ⏰ 10am-midnight

Yacht Club (1, D10)
Like its next-door neighbour the Privilege Club, the Yacht Club attracts a smartly dressed assortment of young locals and visitors. The clubs vie with each other to attract the most chic crowd. You'll need smart casual attire.
✉ **Dukos Beaufort 9** ☎ 081-244 850 ⏰ 11pm-dawn

RETHYMNO

The bar/cafes along **El Venizelou** fill up on summer evenings with pink-skinned tourists, dazed from the burning sun and nursing tropical drinks. The ambience is comfortable but soporific. Rethymno's livelier nightlife is concentrated in the streets around the **Venetian harbour** where a cluster of bars, clubs and discos create a carnival atmosphere. There's not a lot of variety in the nightlife scene; most places are literally grabbing people off the street and cramming them onto the dance floor for a dose of techno and house, but there are a few islands of calm amidst the uproar.

Baja (4, F5)
Formerly a cinema, this huge dance club has hired an attractive multilingual staff in an effort to capture the tourist market. The pirate ship décor is good corny fun and the sounds are contemporary international.
⊠ **Salaminos** ☎ 0831-51 593 ⊘ 11pm-dawn

Club 252 (4, E6)
During the day, the wide terrace is a great place to linger over a coffee. At night Rethymno's twenty-somethings polish themselves up to meet friends and soon-to-be-friends under the stars.
⊠ **Thambergi 1** ⊘ 10am-1am

Delfini
It may be getting passé but Delfini is still the only open-air disco in town, with an unbeatable location on the beach.
⊠ **Venizelou** ☎ 0831-23 365

Figaro (4, G5)
Housed within an ingeniously restored old building, this atmospheric bar attracts a subdued crowd for drinks, snacks and rock music.
⊠ **Venardou 21** ☎ 0831-29 431 ⊘ noon-midnight

Fortezza Disco (4, E6)
Fortezza is the town's showpiece disco. It's big and flashy with 3 bars, a laser show and a well-groomed international crowd that starts drifting in around midnight. Dress smart casual.
⊠ **Nearhou** ⊘ 11pm-dawn

Gounakis Restaurant & Bar (4, G3)
If you love drinking cheap wine and listening to live Cretan folk music, this is the place to go. There's music and impromptu dancing most nights (p. 84).
⊠ **Koroneou 6** ☎ 0831-28 816 ⊘ 8pm-1am

Metropolis NYC
(4, F6) The DJ spins hits from the '60s for a crowd that comes to tank up on cocktails before hitting the discos.
⊠ **Nearhou** ⊘ 7pm-dawn

Nitro Club (4, F6)
In the heart of Rethymno's nightlife district, Nitro is a crowded, friendly dance club with music that leans toward techno early in the evening and Greek later on.
⊠ **Nearhou 26** ☎ 0831-27 205 ⊘ 10pm-dawn

Notes (4, E4)
This quiet bar/cafe with a polished wood bar was opened by a musician who has an excellent selection of Greek music. It's a good place to escape the crowds along El Venizelou.
⊠ **Makedonias 1** ⊘ 10am-midnight

Trapeza (4, F6)
Trapeza is enjoying its moment in the sun as Rethymno's trendiest hangout. The crowd of young professionals who converge on the club each night may move on soon, but right now this is where the action is.
⊠ **Petihaki 2** ⊘ 9pm-dawn

Kick off the night with cocktails at Metropolis NYC

AROUND CRETE

Bachalo
When the summer gets going in Iraklio, clubbers head west to Ammoudara beach and beyond. Bachalo, the hottest disco in the region, generates high-voltage glamour on summer evenings. Dress smart.
✉ **Linoperamata (2, D9), 5km west of Iraklio** ☎ **081-822 120** 🚍 **from the western end of the main road of Ammoudara, follow signs to the disco** ⊘ **June-Sept 11pm-dawn**

The IT Club
This huge, flashy disco with a booming sound system is the centrepiece of the night action in Hersonisos, the nightlife capital of Crete.
✉ **El Venizelou 44, Hersonisos (2, D10)** ⊘ **Apr-Oct 11pm-dawn; weekends only in winter**

New York Music Pub
During the day, New York Music Pub serves drinks, ice cream and snacks on its tables alongside the sea; at night the music gets louder and harder-edged as the dancers move in.
✉ **Ag Paraskevis 30, Hersonisos (2, D10)** ☎ **0897-23 052** ⊘ **Apr-Oct 9am-2am**

Nostos Night Club
When you get tired of lingering over drinks at one of the terrace-cafes along Paleohora's pedestrian streets, head to Nostos to shake your booty in the dance-garden with the locals.
✉ **between El Venizelou & the Old Harbour, Paleohora (2, F2)** ☎ **0823-42 145** ⊘ **6pm-2am**

Paleohora Club
Paleohora's only disco is set well away from the quiet town centre. It's a good place to dance up a storm on a summer evening.
✉ **1.5km north of Paleohora (2, F2), next to Camping Paleohora** ☎ **0823-42 230** ⊘ **Apr-Oct 11pm-4am**

Splendid Cocktail & Dancing Bar
From breakfasts to late-night cocktails and dancing, this music bar does a brisk business, especially at night when the interior is wall-to-wall with locals and visitors.
✉ **Platanias (2, D3)** ☎ **0821-60 346** ⊘ **Apr-Oct 9am-1am**

Utopia
This relaxed cocktail bar attracts people of all ages who enjoy music from the '60s, '70s and '80s.
✉ **Platanias (2, D3)** ☎ **0821-60 033** ⊘ **7pm-2am**

Festivals
Most festivals centre on religious holidays. The Orthodox religion sustained Cretan culture during the many dark centuries of repression, despite numerous and largely futile efforts by the Venetians and Turks to turn the Cretans toward Catholicism and Islam.

Cretans still celebrate **Greek Orthodox holidays** with enthusiasm, though the Orthodox Church of Crete is independent from the Greek Orthodox Church and answers to the Patriarch of Constantinople.

Easter is taken much more seriously than any other religious holiday. On Palm Sunday (the Sunday before Orthodox Easter), worshippers return from church services with a cross woven of palm and myrtle. The Monday evening service is the 'Bridegroom Service' because the priest carries an icon of Christ, the 'bridegroom', through the church. Tuesday is dedicated to Mary Magdalene and Wednesday is the 'Day of Atonement'. On Thursday worshippers mourn for Christ in the evening service and on Good Friday, the symbolic body of Christ is carried through the streets in a funeral procession.

The climax of the week is the Saturday evening service. At midnight all lights are extinguished until the priest appears with a lighted candle and the cry 'Christos Anesti!' (Christ has arisen). He lights each worshipper's candle and people make their way home, trying to keep the candle lit. Fireworks and gunshots herald the start of feasting that lasts through Easter Sunday.

places to stay

Crete has a wide range of accommodation, from simple pensions to luxury resorts. Years of package tourism have resulted in a certain standardisation but most accommodation is relatively good value, depending on the time of year you arrive. **Peak season** is July and August; accommodation fills up and prices are highest. Summers are also hot and bring mosquitoes. The pension that was charming and homey in April can be stifling and buggy in June. Getting a decent night's sleep can override all other considerations in choosing summertime lodging, but the rest of the year you'll have more options.

Neil Setchfield

Neil Setchfield

> **Room Rates**
> Prices are for a double room in high season (July-August) and include all taxes. In May, June and September, prices drop by about 30%; at other times by 50%.
>
> | | |
> |---|---|
> | $ | 5000-11,000 dr |
> | $$ | 12,000-25,000 dr |
> | $$$ | 26,000-40,000 dr |
> | $$$$ | over 40,000 dr |

Hotel Panorama in Agios Nikolaos

Staying in old **Venetian mansions** is one of the great pleasures of the Cretan accommodation scene. In the old quarters of Hania and Rethymno, enterprising families have taken over decaying mansions, restored them and turned them into elegant hotels. More modest structures have become 'rent rooms' offering wonderful local hospitality. The difference between a hotel and rent rooms is in the common areas. Hotels must offer a lounge and a breakfast option; rent rooms rarely have breakfast facilities but often install a fridge and hot plate in the room or even kitchenettes.

A huge investment of land and money has gone into the development of first-class and luxury **resorts** along the north coast. Many of these resorts are designed as small towns with shopping, a choice of restaurants, bars, entertainment, sports activities, childcare facilities and any other service to keep guests on the premises and spending money. There's always an outdoor swimming pool and sometimes an indoor pool, sauna and fitness centre. You'll usually find a children's wading pond and playground, tennis courts and water-sports centre.

Double rooms are invariably large and twin-bedded with en-suite bathrooms. Often there's a higher charge for rooms with balconies, sea views or air-con but otherwise the rooms are identical. Triples and suites are available for families, while children under 12 are often lodged free or half-price.

In contrast to town hotels that are generally open all year, most resorts are only open from March or April to October or November.

AGIOS NIKOLAOS

As Agios Nikolaos receives few guests in the winter, most hotels close. The only establishments open all year are the Doxa and Dias hotels. The luxury resorts are along the beach road running north between the town centre and Elounda.

Elena (3, J1) $
A solid-value option in the centre of town, Elena offers large, airy rooms equipped with the basics but no extras. Everything is in working order but don't expect much in the way of decoration.
✉ Minoos 15 ☎ 0841-28 189; fax 0841-24 102 ✕ breakfast room

Hotel Apollon (3, J1) $$
Conveniently located in the centre of town near Kitroplatia beach, the Apollon is a large, modern hotel offering rooms with balcony, phone, fridge and air-conditioning. There's also a small pool and a games room with a pool table. Prices include a buffet breakfast.
✉ Kapetanaki 9 ☎ 0841-23 023; fax 0841-28 939 ✆ www. forthnet.gr/internetcity/ hotels/apollon ✕ bar, breakfast room

Hotel Coral (3, E1) $$
On the edge of Ammoudi beach, the Coral Hotel is large and modern, offering comfortable rooms with TV and balcony. There's also a sauna, outdoor swimming pool and water-sports centre. Prices include buffet breakfast.
✉ Akti Koundourou ☎ 0841-28 363/367; fax 0841-28 754 ✕ restaurant, bar

Hotel Dias (3, K1) $
This small hotel in the town centre is decorated in a traditional style and offers rooms with phone, TV, fridge and hair-dryer. Some rooms have balconies and air-con on demand.
✉ Latous 6 ☎ 0841-28 263/4 ✕ bar, breakfast room

Hotel Doxa (3, J2) $
The plant-filled lobby sets a homey tone for this hotel which also boasts an attractive terrace for breakfast or drinks. Rooms are small but inviting and equipped with phone and balcony.
✉ Idomeneos 7 ☎ 0841-24 214; fax 0841-24 614

Hotel Mariella (3, K1) $
The lobby isn't much in this small, family-run hotel, but the clean white rooms are cheerful and many have balconies. The hotel is conveniently located on a busy commercial street; front rooms can be noisy during the day but the area calms down at night when the action shifts to bars around the port.
✉ Latous 4 ☎ 0841-28 639 ✕ breakfast room

Hotel Panorama (3, F4) $$
The Panorama is named for the views it offers of Agios Nikolaos' harbour and bay. The hotel has recently been renovated and now has air-con in its attractive, Mediterranean-style rooms. If you can't get a room with a balcony and sea view, console yourself with the view from the rooftop garden.
✉ Sarolidi 2 ☎ 0841-28 890; fax 0841-27 268 ✕ breakfast room, bar

Katerina Pension (3, F2) $$
One of the best pensions in Agios Nikolaos, Katerina is

At the water's edge: Hotel Coral

Neil Setchfield

in an old house on a quiet, residential street. The enclosed garden is a delight and some rooms have their own balcony.
✉ **Koraka 33** ☎ **0841-22 766**

Minos Beach Hotel & Bungalows $$$$

This hotel-bungalow complex 2km north of Agios Nikolaos has everything a luxury-seeker could want. Although built in 1962 as the opening salvo in Agios Nikolaos' assault on global tourism, it has been scrupulously maintained and updated. The exquisitely decorated bungalows are on a rocky cove with a few sandy beaches; there's a pool and all conceivable water-sports activities. Prices include buffet breakfast.

> **Going Solo**
>
> Because most visitors arrive as couples or families on an air-package, there has been no incentive to build single rooms which are now nearly nonexistent on the island. Generally, the single price is about 75% of the double price but in peak season, when the demand for rooms is high, single travellers may be forced to pay the full price of a double room.

✉ **2km north of Agios Nikolaos** ☎ **0841-22 345/349; fax 0841-22 548** @ **www.forthnet.gr/internetcity/hotels/minosb/** 🚌 **regular local buses from Plateia Venizelou** ✕ **3 bars, 2 restaurants, snack bar**

Miramare Hotel $$$

About 1km south of the town centre, the Miramare has been attractively landscaped into a hillside. The skilfully decorated rooms are outfitted with air-con on demand, satellite TV, fridge, phone and balcony. Try to get a room near the top of the hill for the stunning sea views. There's a swimming pool, tennis courts and fitness centre. Prices include buffet breakfast.
✉ **Gargadoros** ☎ **0841-23 875; fax 0841-24 164** @ **mare@agn.forthnet.gr** ✕ **bar, taverna, restaurant**

HANIA

Hania's Venetian quarter is chock-full of family-run hotels and pensions housed in restored Venetian buildings. The western end of the harbour is a good place to look but it can be noisy at night. Most hotels in town are open all year. Resorts are along the strip of beach west of the town centre.

Akasti $

This new hotel, across the road from tiny swimming coves, offers simple but large rooms with phone, fridge and balcony. The roof-terrace bar/dining room has a view of the sea and there are stores nearby to pick up supplies.
✉ **Kalamaki, 5km west of Hania** ☎ **0821-31 352; fax 0821-33 101** ✕ **restaurant/bar**

Amfora Hotel (5, E3) $$

Located in an immaculately restored Venetian mansion with rooms around a court-

yard, the Amfora is Hania's most historically evocative hotel. There's no elevator and no air-con but the rooms are elegantly decorated and some have views of the harbour. Front rooms can be noisy in summer. Prices include buffet breakfast.
✉ **Parados Theotokopoulou 2** ☎ **0821-93 224/226; fax 0821-93 224/226** ✕ **restaurant**

Casa Delfino (5, E3) $$$

This modernised 17th-century mansion features a splendid courtyard of tradi-

Niki Setchfield

Monastiri Pension

tionally patterned cobblestones and 19 individually decorated suites. All have

air-con, satellite TV, phone, hair-dryer, minibar and safe. Some suites have spas and business travellers will appreciate the modem ports. Prices include buffet breakfast.
✉ **Theofanous 7** ☎ 0821-93 098; fax 0821-96 500 @ casadel@cha.forthnet.gr ✗ wine bar

Danaos $$
The best feature of this rather bland, modern hotel is its location across the road from Nea Hora beach. The functional rooms have balconies and phones. The price range given is for rooms with a sea view.
✉ **Akti Papanikoli, Nea Hora** ☎ 0821-96 021; fax 0821-96 022 ✗ terrace restaurant/bar

Kastelli (5, E6) $$
At the quieter eastern end of the harbour, Kastelli has singles, doubles and renovated apartments with high ceilings, white walls and pine floors. There's no TV or phone but some rooms have attractive views.
✉ **Kanevaro 39** ☎ 0821-57 057; fax 0821-45 314

Palazzo Hotel

Kydon Hotel (5, H5) $$$
Just outside the old town, Kydon is slick, modern and comfortable. The carpeted rooms are soundproof and have satellite TV, fridge, safe, hair-dryer and modem port. There's air-con on demand plus free parking. Prices include buffet breakfast.
✉ **Giannari** ☎ 0821-52 280; fax 0821-51 790 @ kydon@cha.forthnet.gr ✗ restaurant, coffee shop

Monastiri Pension (5, E6) $
Monastiri Pension has a great setting right next to the ruins of the monastery of Santa Maria de Miracolioco, in the heart of the Old Town near the Venetian Arsenal. Rooms are simple with shared bathrooms; some rooms have a sea view. There's a convenient communal kitchen for preparing light meals.
✉ **Ag Markou 18** ☎ 0821-54 776

Nostos Pension (5, F3) $$
Mixing Venetian style and modern fixtures, this 600-year-old building has been modelled into classy, split-level rooms and units, all with kitchen and bathroom. Try to get a room in front for the view of the harbour.
✉ **Zambeliou 42-46** ☎ 0821-94 740; fax 0821-54 502

Palazzo Hotel (5, E3) $$
On a pedestrian street at the western end of the old harbour, the Palazzo is a restored mansion with wrought-iron balconies and wood shutters. The pine-floored rooms have air-con,

Pension Nora

fridge, safe and phone, but there's no elevator.
✉ **Theotokopoulou 54** ☎ 0821-93 227; fax 0821-93 229

Pension Nora (5, D3) $
Located in a restored Turkish building, Pension Nora has large rooms attractively outfitted with Cretan rugs, iron lamps and wood furniture. The composer Mikis Theodorakis reputedly lodged here when he was a soldier. In an unusual arrangement, each room has its own locked toilet/shower cubicle in the hall.
✉ **Theotokopoulou 60** ☎ 0821-72 225; fax 0821-72 225

Pension Theresa (5, E3) $$
Three storeys of antiques-stocked rooms in a creaky old house make Pension Theresa the most atmospheric pension in Hania. If you don't snag a room with a view, there's always the stunning vista from the rooftop terrace.
✉ **Angelou 2** ☎ 0821-92 798; fax 0821-92 798

Porto Veneziano $$$
On the harbour's eastern

edge, this stylish and comfortable hotel offers large rooms with TV, phone and air-con. The light, fresh decoration is cheerful and there's an interior garden for relaxing. Prices include buffet breakfast.

✉ **Old Venetian Harbour** ☎ **0821-27 100; fax 0821-27 105** @ **portoven@otenet.gr; www.aegean.ch/hotels/ portoven.htm** ✗ **café/bar, taverna**

Vranas Studios
(5, F5)   **$$**
Vranas Studios is on a lively pedestrian street and has spacious, immaculate studios with kitchenettes. All rooms have polished timber floors, balcony, TV and phone and you can have air-con for a supplement. The price range given is for August; figure on at least 40% less at any other time.
✉ **Ag Deka 10** ☎ **0821-58 618; fax 0821-58 618**

Pension Theresa

IRAKLIO

As it's the island's capital and business centre, Iraklio's accommodation is geared toward the needs of business travellers. Hotels tend to be bland but they are clustered in the centre of town, convenient to public transport. The beach resort closest to Iraklio is **Ammoudara**, 2km west of town. You'll find the top-end resorts stretching to Ammoudara in the west and **Hersonisos** in the east. Hotels in town are open all year but most beach resorts are only open from March to November.

Astoria Hotel
(1, F8)   **$$$**
Astoria is the business-person's choice. It's in the thick of the action on Plateia Eleftherias, convenient to all public transport and equipped with a rooftop swimming pool. The luxurious rooms are outfitted with air-con on demand, hair-dryer, cosmetics, TV (international channels) and phone. Prices include buffet breakfast.
✉ **Plateia Eleftherias 11** ☎ **081-343 080; fax 081-229 078** @ **astoria@her.forthnet.gr** ✗ **café, pool bar, snack bar, restaurant**

Atlantis Hotel
(1, D9)   **$$$**
Located on a quiet street near the harbour, this gleaming, modern hotel has an indoor swimming pool,

health club, sauna and solarium. The rooms are spacious and well-appointed with air-con on demand, TV (no English-language stations), phone, bathtub and double-glazed windows to ensure quiet. Prices include buffet breakfast.
✉ **Igias 2** ☎ **081-22 9103/4023; fax 081-22 6265** @ **reserv_atl@atl.**

grecotel.gr ✗ **bar, restaurant, snack bar**

Atrion Hotel
(1, C5)   **$$**
Atrion is a businesslike establishment with few concessions to frivolity. The large, well-furnished rooms have air-con on demand, TV with international stations and modern

The Air-Con Con
From June to August temperatures hover in the 90s and don't come down much at night. Coastal cities can also be extremely humid. The concept of fans has never caught on and hotels with air-con try to keep their utility bills down by limiting it to certain hours, sometimes the very hours when guests are on the beach! The best arrangement is air-con on demand, which allows you to choose your own cooling schedule. If the air-con is centrally regulated, find out how many hours a day and during which hours the room will be cooled.

bathrooms, but the hotel's most attractive feature is the enclosed garden terrace. Prices include buffet breakfast.

✉ **Chronaki 9** ☎ 081-229 225; fax 081-223 292 ✕ bar, restaurant

El Greco (1, E5) $$

Near the Morosini fountain, the no-nonsense El Greco has a large, bland lobby which seems designed to discourage lingering. No one would accuse the hotel of over-decorating its rooms but they are in decent shape and some have TV and air-con. The location is good. Breakfast is included.

✉ **1821 street, No 4** ☎ 081-281 071; fax 081-281 072 ✕ bar, snack bar, breakfast room

Galaxy Hotel $$$

Although not in the town centre, Galaxy offers a lot of amenities. There's a swimming pool large enough to swim laps, a sauna and very comfortable rooms with air-con on demand, TV with international stations, phone, hair-

Hotel Ilaira

dryer, safe and balcony. Buffet breakfast is included.

✉ **Demokratias 67** ☎ 081-238 812; fax 081-211 211 ❸ galaxyir@otenet.gr ✕ bar, snack bar, restaurant

Hotel Ilaira (1, C8) $$

The best feature of Hotel Ilaira is the rooftop terrace with its panoramic view of the ports and fortress. The pleasant stucco and timber rooms have phone and shower; some have TV and others have small balconies with sea views.

✉ **Ariadnis 1** ☎ 081-227 103/125; fax 081-242 367 ✕ rooftop bar

Hotel Irini (1, C8) $$

This modern establishment with parking facilities has 59 large, airy rooms with TV (only local stations), radio, phone and air-con. It's well located in the centre of town and most of the Mediterranean-style rooms have balconies with plants and flowers. The taverna downstairs has long opening hours. Prices include breakfast.

✉ **Idomeneos 4** ☎ 081-226 561; fax 081-226 407 ✕ breakfast room/bar

Hotel Kastro (1, C5) $$

Hotel Kastro has comfortable amenities including a great rooftop terrace with chairs for sunbathing. Some of the rooms have corner balconies with sea views; all rooms are large and have phone and air-con. Some have TV. Prices include breakfast.

✉ **Theotokopoulou 22** ☎ 081-284 185/285 020; fax 081-223 622 ✕ breakfast room

Olympic Hotel

Hotel Kronos (1, B6) $

Hotel Kronos is as close to the sea as you can get in Iraklio without getting wet. The large, twin-bedded rooms are in excellent condition, with sparkling tile floors and white walls. All rooms have balconies (some with sea views) and double-glazed windows keep out traffic noise from the road below.

✉ **Venizelou 2** ☎ 081-282 240; fax 081-285 853 ✕ breakfast room, bar

Hotel Lato (1, C8) $$$

Completely renovated in 1995, this sleek hotel overlooking the fortress offers excellent value. The comfortable rooms have air-con on demand, TV with international stations, phone, radio and balconies with sea views. There's also a conference room and parking facilities. Prices include buffet breakfast.

✉ **Epimendou 15** ☎ 081-228 103 fax 081-240 350 ❸ lato@her.forthnet.gr; www.forthnet.gr/lato ✕ bar, snack bar

Hotel Mirabello
(1, C5) **S**
This friendly hotel is on a quiet street in the centre of town. Rooms are simple but well-tended. Some have private bathrooms; in others you'll share a bathroom but the communal facilities are immaculate.

Try to get a room with a balcony.
✉ **Theotokopoulou 20**
☎ **081-285 052/852**

Olympic (1, G6) **SS**
Although bland, the large Olympic offers a sunny rooftop garden and a central location. The large

rooms are in good condition and equipped with phones. Prices include breakfast.
✉ **Plateia Kornarou**
☎ **081-288 861; fax 081-222 512**
@ **galaxyir@otenet.gr**
✗ **bar, breakfast room**

RETHYMNO

Rethymno's accommodation scene has something for everyone. Because it's a dynamic commercial centre, many hotels are open all year. Those who want to lounge around a resort should head east from the town centre to find an endless string of hotels. Within the town centre, there's plenty of restored mansions and friendly pensions to help immerse yourself in the town's fascinating history.

Astali **SS**
This new hotel hadn't got around to installing TVs and phones in the rooms but it hardly matters when the rooms are so spiffy and modern. The bathrooms are state-of-the-art and there's air-con. Prices include buffet breakfast.
✉ **Papandreou 1** ☎ **0831-24 721; fax 0831-30 8310**

Grecotel Creta Palace **SSSS**
Like all of Rethymno's luxury establishments, the

Hotel Ideon

Grecotel Creta Palace is outside town on the beach. There are 2 outdoor pools and one indoor, a children's playground, tennis courts, a fitness club and all watersports facilities. The rooms have air-con on demand, TV with international stations and phone.
✉ **Missira (2, E6), 4km east of Rethymno** ☎ **0831-55 181; fax 0831-54 085** @ **www.2m.hol.gr/grecotel** 🚌 **buses every ½hr from Rethymno centre** ✗ **3 bars, cafeteria, restaurant, taverna**

Hotel Fortezza
(4, F4) **SS**
This hotel is an oasis of calm in a busy neighbourhood. Housed in a refurbished old building in the heart of the Old Town, the tastefully furnished rooms have TV, phone and air-con on demand. After a day of roaming Rethymno, it's pleasant to relax by the hotel swimming pool. Prices include buffet breakfast.
✉ **Melissinou 16** ☎

0831-55 551/552 or 23 828; fax 0831-54 073 ✗ **snack bar, restaurant**

Hotel Ideon (4, E5) SS
If you don't feel like walking all the way to the beach, you can cool off in Ideon's swimming pool. Other amenities in this polished establishment include rooms with air-con, safe, radio, phone and balcony. Prices include buffet breakfast.
✉ **Plastira 10** ☎ **0831-28 667; fax 0831-28 670** ✗ **restaurant, snack bar, bar**

Hotel Veneto
(4, G4) **SSS**
The oldest part of this historic hotel dates from the 15th century and it has preserved many traditional features without sacrificing modern comforts. The eye-catching rooms with polished timber floors and ceilings also have air-con, TV, phone, safe and kitchenette.
✉ **Epimenidou 4** ☎ **0831-56 634;**

Rent Rooms Sea View

Neil Setchfield

fax 0831-56 635
✉ veneto@interkriti.gr
✗ bar, restaurant

Kyma Beach   **$$$**
This hotel is a favourite with package tours largely because of its excellent location just across from the beach and within walking distance of the town centre. Most rooms have air-con, TV and phone and there's a small pool. Prices include buffet breakfast.
✉ S Venizelou 1 ☎ 0831-55 503; fax 0831-27 746 ✗ restaurant, cocktail bar, pool bar

Lefteris Papadakis Rooms (4, E4)   **$**
Tranquillity is not the selling point here but if you want to be in the centre of Rethymno's nightlife you've come to the right place. All rooms are pleasant; the front rooms have stunning sea views although they can be noisy at night. There are some rooms with shared bath.
✉ Plastira 26 ☎ 0831-23 803

Olga's Pension (4, G5)   **$**
This friendly establishment

is tucked away on the touristy but colourful Souliou street. A network of terraces, all bursting with greenery, connects the rooms, some with bath and sea views.
✉ Souliou 57 ☎ 0831-28 665

Park Hotel (4, H4)   **$$**
The rooms here are comfortable, with air-con, TV, phone, sound-proofing and balconies affording a view of the municipal park. The only missing ingredient is an elevator. Prices include breakfast.
✉ Gavril 9 ☎ 0831-29 958

Rent Rooms Garden (4, G4)   **$$**
On a quiet street in Rethymno's Old Town, this impeccably maintained 600-year-old Venetian house retains many of its original features including impressive doors and a gorgeous grape-arboured garden. The rooms are simple, comfortable and tasteful.
✉ Nikiforou Foka 82 ☎ 0831-28 586

Rent Rooms Sea View (4, H6)   **$**
This delightful pension has only 6 studio apartments but each one is fresh and cheerful. The best part is that you're right across the street from the beach; the worst part is that the front rooms can be noisy at night.
✉ El Venizelou 45 ☎ 0831-51 981; fax 0831-51 062 ✉ elotia@ret. forthnet.gr; www. forthnet.gr/elotia

Rooms for Rent Anda (4, H4)   **$**
This pension is a great choice if you have kids

Sticker Price
By law, the price of a room must be displayed in the room. The displayed prices are registered with the National Tourism Office and reflect the maximum that the hotel can charge for the room during specified seasons.

There are several ways to avoid paying 'sticker price'. Buying an air-and-accommodation package from a travel agency is invariably cheaper than making your own bookings. Travel agencies block-book and obtain huge discounts on the rooms. If you turn up on your own, be prepared to bargain, especially if you arrive out of peak season or intend to stay more than one night. Crete has overbuilt in the last decade and, except in August, there are usually many more hotel rooms than people to fill them.

because it's just a short walk from Rethymno's municipal park. The prettily furnished rooms have private bathrooms but no other amenities, although the owner will gladly help you with anything you need.

✉ Nikiforou Foka 33
☎ 0831-23 479

**Rooms to Rent
Barbara Dolomaki**
(4, E5) $
This rambling pension in the middle of Rethymno's

nightlife district has comfortable rooms with and without kitchenettes. The rooms with kitchenettes are larger and newly refurbished.
✉ Thambergi 14 ☎ 0831-24 581

AROUND CRETE

Hotels and pensions in Crete tend to cluster along the coast since that's where the tourists are. Accommodation in the interior is limited. Family-run 'rent rooms' places crop up in interior towns and villages but hotels are scarce. Outside of the tourist centres on the north coast, accommodation is strictly seasonal. Finding a place to stay between November and March can be a real problem.

Elounda Beach Hotel & Villas $$$$
One of the world's great luxury resorts, the Elounda Beach offers pampering on a major scale. The rooms run the gamut from `simple' affairs with fresh flowers, bathrobes, twice-daily maid service and bathrooms outfitted with spa and TV, to royal suites with private indoor swimming pool, personal fitness trainer, butler, secretary and cook. There are also bungalows with a private outdoor swimming pool and platform on the sea.
✉ Elounda (2, D12) ☎ 0841-41 412; fax 0841-41 373 ❷ elohotel@ eloundabeach.gr; www.eloundabeach.gr 🚌 regular buses from Agios Nikolaos ✖ 4 restaurants, 3 bars, nightclub

Grecotel Agapi Beach $$$
Although technically not a luxury establishment, this chain hotel delivers a lot of comfort for the price. The sprawling, manicured grounds border Ammoudara beach and contain an enormous swimming pool, a smaller heated pool, a chil-

dren's playground, tennis courts and a water-sports centre. Rooms have all the amenities and some have magnificent views of the beach. The Grecotel chain also has an innovative environmental program. Prices include buffet breakfast.
✉ N Stadion, Ammoudara beach (2, D9) ☎ 081-250 502; fax 081-258 731 🚌 regular city buses from Iraklio ✖ kafeneion, 2 bars, taverna, disco, restaurant

Hotel Idi $$
Outside the mountain town of Zaros, surrounded by

The playground in front of the Petra Mare Hotel, Ierapetra

Neil Setchfield

trees and greenery, the Idi is a restful escape from the crowded coast. The pleasant, traditional rooms have air-con and there's a swimming pool, tennis courts and hiking in the surrounding hills. Prices include buffet breakfast.

✉ **Zaros (2, F8)** ☎ **0894-31 301; fax 0894-31 511** @ **votomos@ otenet.gr** 🚌 **3 daily buses from Iraklio** 🚗 **take the main road south from Iraklio and turn west at Agia Varvara** ✕ **restaurant, cafe, bar**

Itanos Hotel $$

With a conspicuous waterfront location and a popular terrace restaurant, Itanos is hard to miss. The comfortable rooms are outfitted with air-con on demand, satellite TV, balconies and sound-proofing for a tranquil night's sleep. Special rooms are available for disabled travellers.

✉ **Karamanli 4, Sitia (2, E14)** ☎ **0843-22 900; fax 0843-22 915** @ **www.forthnet.gr/ internetcity/hotels/ itanos** ✕ **bar, restaurant**

Komis Studios $$$

Ecologically sound and aesthetically pleasing, this complex on the beach offers 3-level apartments exquisitely decorated in a rustic style but with the comforts of air-con, phone and TV. The units use wind and solar power; the sewage is treated biologically and the excellent restaurant uses local produce.

✉ **Keratokambos (2, F11)** ☎ **0895-51 390; fax 0895-51 393** ✕ **restaurant/bar**

Oriental Bay Rooms $

Accommodation is basic in Paleohora but Oriental Bay Rooms, at the northern end of the pebble beach, offers a good deal. The rooms are large and well-maintained and the ceiling fans give welcome relief in sticky summer heat. The shady terrace-restaurant overlooking the sea serves decent meals and is a pleasant place to hang out.

✉ **Paleohora (2, F2)** ☎ **0823-41 076** ✕ **restaurant/bar**

Petra Mare Hotel $$$

A few km east of Ierapetra, the beachside Petra Mare is architecturally uninspiring but it has an indoor and outdoor pool, tennis courts, sauna, fitness centre, children's play area and water-sports centre. Rooms have air-con, TV and phone. Prices include buffet breakfast.

✉ **Filotheou A, Ierapetra (2, F12)** ☎ **0842-23 341/9; fax 0842-23 350** @ **www. forthnet.gr/internetcity/ hotels/petramare** ✕ **2 bars, restaurant, cafe, taverna**

Royal Mare Village $$$$

With almost 400 newly built bungalows, the vast Royal Mare is more a metropolis-on-the-sea than a village. With 2 children's pools, 2 outdoor pools, an indoor pool, tennis courts, water sports, a children's playground, fitness centre, volleyball, archery and a nightclub, you'll never run out of things to do. The most outstanding feature is the Thalasso Centre, the most modern and best-equipped water wonderland in Crete.

✉ **Hersonisos (2, D10)** ☎ **0897-25 025; fax 0897-21 664** @ **market ing@aldemar.gr; www. aldemar.gr** ✕ **bars, restaurants, coffee shop, taverna**

Itanos Hotel – right on Sitia's waterfront

Neil Setchfield

facts for the visitor

PRE-DEPARTURE 108

Travel Requirements 108
Tourist Information Abroad 108
Climate & When to Go 108

ARRIVAL & DEPARTURE 109

Air 109
Customs 109
Duty Free 110
Departure Tax 110

GETTING AROUND 110

Bus 110
Taxi 110
Boat 110
Car & Motorcycle 111

PRACTICAL INFORMATION 112

Tourist Information 112
Embassies 113

Money 113
Tipping 113
Discounts 113
Opening Hours 113
Public Holidays 114
Time 114
Electricity 114
Weights & Measures 114
Post 114
Telephone 115
Email/www 115
Newspapers & Magazines 115
Radio 116
TV 116
Photography & Video 116
Health 116
Toilets 117
Emergency Numbers 117
Safety Concerns 117
Women Travellers 117
Gay & Lesbian Travellers 117
Disabled Travellers 117
Language 118
Glossary 120
Conversion Table 121

Traditional lacemaking with a modern theme, Vrises

PRE-DEPARTURE
Travel Requirements

Australians, Canadians, New Zealanders, South Africans and US citizens with a valid passport (valid for 6 months from date of entry) can stay visa-free for up to three months but need to produce an onward ticket. An AIDS test is required for performing artists and students on Greek scholarships. EU citizens can enter with their identity cards.

Immunisations
No jabs are required for travel to Greece but a yellow fever vaccination certificate is required if you are coming from an infected area.

Travel Insurance
Get a policy covering theft, loss and medical problems. Don't skim over the small print: some policies exclude 'dangerous activities', such as scuba diving, motorcycling and even trekking.

Driving Licence & Permit
EU citizens can use their normal licence. Citizens of other countries are told to get an International Driving Permit but in practice this requirement is rarely enforced and a valid driving licence is sufficient.

Keeping Copies
Keep photocopies of important documents with you, separate from the originals, and leave a copy at home.

You can also store details of documents in Lonely Planet's free online Travel Vault, password-protected and accessible worldwide. See www.ekno.lonelyplanet.com.

Tourist Information Abroad

The Greek National Tourist Organisation (GNTO) can be contacted in:

Australia & New Zealand
51 Pitt St, Sydney NSW 2000 (☎ 02-9241 1663)

Canada
1300 Bay St, Toronto, Ontario M5R 3K8 (☎ 416-968 2220); 1233 rue de la Montagne, Suite 101, Montreal, Quebec H3G 1Z2 (☎ 514-871 1535)

UK
4 Conduit St, London WlR DOJ (☎ 071-734 5997)

USA
Olympic Tower, 645 Fifth Ave, New York, NY 10022 (☎ 212-421 5777)

Climate & When to Go

Crete has a Mediterranean climate, with hot, dry summers and mild winters (although you'll see snow on the mountains). It also stays warm the longest of all the Greek islands – you can swim off its southern coast from mid-April to November.

The worst time to visit Crete is when everyone else visits – from mid-June to the end of August. Prices are highest, beaches are crowded and the heat can be overpowering. In July and August, the Aegean's notorious *meltemi* wind, which blows from the north, can provide relief from the heat but make beach life unpleasant.

Wildflowers such as anemones

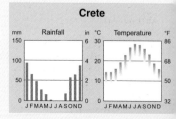

Crete

Rainfall — mm / in · Temperature — °C / °F
J F M A M J J A S O N D

and orchids are at their best in March and April which is also a good time for outdoor activities such as trekking and biking. The island starts to heat up in late-May and doesn't cool down until September. You can still swim in September but by October it's usually too chilly except on the southern coast.

Many hotels shut down in winter so accommodation can be a problem but it's a good time to discover traditional village life since everyone is hard at work on the olive harvest.

ARRIVAL & DEPARTURE

There's no shortage of direct charter flights between Crete and the UK and Europe, but the only direct scheduled flight is between Frankfurt and Iraklio. If you're coming from Australia, New Zealand, North America or South Africa you'll have to go through Athens.

There are no direct international boat connections to Crete, but there are daily connections to Piraeus from Iraklio, Hania and Rethymno and 3 ferries a week from Iraklio to Thessaloniki.

Air

Iraklio

Nikos Kazantzakis airport is 4.8km east of Iraklio's city centre. There is only one terminal and it has a post office, bank, left luggage service and is wheelchair accessible.

Inquiries/Flight Info	☎ 081-228 402
Olympic Airways	☎ 081-22 9191
Air Greece	☎ 081-33 0729
	or 33 0739
Car Park Info	☎ 081-228 402

Airport Access Bus No 1 travels to/from the airport every 15 minutes between 6am and 1am (170 dr). It leaves the city from outside the Astoria Hotel on Plateia Eleftherias. A taxi to/from the airport costs 1500 dr.

For car hire, Hertz, Eurodollar, Europcar and Reliable are some of the companies with offices at the airport. There's also a Motor Club office for renting motorcycles.

Hania

Hania's airport, 14km east of the city centre, handles only domestic flights. There's no left-luggage service.

Inquiries/Flight Info	☎ 0821-63 264
Olympic Airways	☎ 0821-57 701
Air Greece	☎ 0821-66 304
Car Park Info	☎ 0821-63 264

Airport Access A taxi to/from the airport costs 3000 dr. For car hire, Hertz and Avis are available.

Customs

Customs authorities use the red and green system. Visitors move down the green lane if they have nothing to declare, or follow the red lane if they have articles to declare. If you're taking medication make sure you get a supporting statement from your doctor. Codeine, common in headache preparations, is banned in Greece.

When leaving Greece, you must declare art and antiques, and get an export permit for antiquities (anything over 100 years old). Taking out antiquities without permission is a crime second only to drug smuggling in Greece. To apply for an export permit, contact the Antique Dealers & Private Collections Section, The Archaeological Service, Polignotou 13, Athens.

Duty Free

You can bring in 200 cigarettes or 50 cigars, 1L of spirits or 2L of wine, 50g of perfume and 250ml of eau de cologne.

Departure Tax

An airport tax for all international departures is included in the price of the ticket. Port taxes vary from 1500-5000 dr, depending on the port.

GETTING AROUND

Bus

Regular and reliable buses link the major northern towns from Kastelli-Kissamos to Sitia. These buses are generally in good shape and some are even air-conditioned. Most buses use the highway but at least 1 or 2 buses each day use the old roads. This trip is more scenic but takes much longer so ask before you buy the ticket. The service running between the north-coast towns and resorts and places of interest on the south coast, via the inland mountain villages, is not so frequent.

In major towns it's best to buy your ticket at the station to make sure you have a seat but if you board at a stop along the way you buy the ticket from the driver. When you buy a bus ticket, you will be given a seat number (look on the ticket). The number is on the back of the bus seat. Keep the ticket: it'll be checked a few times en route. Bus stations in major towns keep long opening hours and are a good source of information.

Local city buses operating from Iraklio, Rethymno and Hania are designed to take people back and forth from the city to the suburbs and are not really practical for getting around the cities themselves. They are cheap and reliable if not terribly comfortable.

Taxi

Taxis are widely available in Crete, except in remote villages, and are relatively cheap by European standards. Large towns have taxi stands that post a list of taxi prices to outlying destinations, which removes any anxiety about over-charging. Otherwise you pay what's on the meter.

You can negotiate with taxis to take you sightseeing for the day using the following prices as a guide: flagfall is 200 dr followed by 62 dr per km (120 dr per km outside town or between midnight and 5am). There's a 300 dr surcharge when the taxi is hired at an airport and a 150 dr surcharge if the taxi is hired at a bus station or port. Each piece of luggage weighing more than 10kg carries a surcharge of 50 dr and there's a surcharge of 300 dr for radio taxis.

If your destination is at the end of a bumpy unpaved road you'll pay considerably more – if you can find a taxi to take you there at all.

Boat

Although there are no boats plying the waters off Crete's north coast, boat travel is a pleasant way to experience the south coast. In summer, daily boats from Paleohora to Hora Sfakion via Agia Roumeli,

Sougia and Loutro offer wonderful coastal views. If you plan to visit Elafonisi, the boat from Paleohora is much more relaxing than the bus from Hania.

Car Ferry

Daily car ferries travel between Piraeus and Hania or Iraklio but transporting your car is considerably more expensive than travelling as a passenger. To transport a car up to 4.25m long costs 17,700 dr, in addition to 5400 dr per passenger. It's wise to reserve ahead if you'll be taking your car, especially if you're travelling in the high season.

Car & Motorcycle

A 4-lane national highway skirts the north coast from Hania in the west to Agios Nikolaos in the east, and is being extended further west to Kastelli-Kissamos.

Few would be surprised to learn that Greece has one of the highest road-fatality rates in Europe – it's a good place to practise your defensive driving skills! Overtaking is the biggest cause of accidents so as a visitor you should familiarise yourself with the rules of the road. Driving in the major cities is a nightmare of erratic one-way streets and irregularly enforced parking rules. Cars are not towed but parking tickets can be expensive. Parking for the disabled is a rarity.

Extreme caution should be exercised when travelling by motorcycle. Roads change without warning from smooth and paved to cracked and pothole-ridden. Watch your speed. Greece is not the best place for novice motorcyclists: many tourists have accidents every year. Experienced motorcyclists will find a lightweight enduro motorcycle 400-600 cc ideal for negotiating Crete's roads.

Petrol is pricey and becomes even more so the farther you are from a main city. Super usually costs 212-235 dr per litre, unleaded is 200-225 dr and diesel is about 160 dr.

Road Rules

Highways and major roads are divided into 4 lanes. You should drive near but not in the right lane; pull into the right lane to allow the car behind you to pass. Seatbelts must be worn in front and back seats. You must travel with a first-aid kit, fire extinguisher and warning triangle. Carrying cans of petrol is banned. Motorcyclists driving bikes of 50cc or more must wear helmets.

Speed Limits For cars, the limit is 120km/h on highways, 90km/h on other roads and 50km/h in built-up areas. For motorcycles, it's 70km/h (up to 100cc), 90km/h (above 100cc).

Drink Driving A blood-alcohol limit of 0.05% will incur a penalty, while 0.08% is a criminal offence.

Car Rental

Hiring a car in Greece is more expensive than in other European countries but the prices have come down recently due to an increasingly competitive environment. It pays to shop around, especially if you're renting a car for a week or more. Although major international companies such as Hertz, Budget and Europcar have offices everywhere, you'll usually get a better deal if you rent from a local company.

Motorcycle & Moped Rental

Motorbikes and mopeds are available for hire wherever there are tourists. Before hiring them, make sure you check the vehicles thoroughly, especially the brakes, as many bikes haven't been well maintained. When you rent a moped, tell the shop where you'll be going to ensure that your vehicle has enough power to get you up Crete's steep hills. Make sure your travel insurance is adequate (see Travel Requirements).

PRACTICAL INFORMATION
Tourist Information

The tourist offices listed below vary widely in the services they provide. The most comprehensive services are offered in Hania and Agios Nikolaos; in other places you'll usually get more information from a local travel agency. Tourist offices will not book excursions, hotel rooms or sell boat tickets but usually have listings of local events.

Ellinikos Organismos Tourismou (EOT)
The EOT is the local version of the GNTO.

Hania
Kriari 40 (☎ 0821- 92 943, fax 92 624), Mon-Fri 7.30am-2.30pm. This helpful office has the latest information about the Samaria Gorge and boat schedules along the south coast.

Iraklio
Xanthoudidou 1 (☎ 0821-22 8225/6081/8203, fax 22 6020), Mon-Fri 8am-2.30pm, weekends in high season. The staff at the information desk are often work-experience students from a local tourism training college. They can give you photocopied lists of ferry and bus schedules, as well as a map.

Municipal Tourist Offices
These offices perform much the same function as their EOT counterparts.

Agios Nikolaos
At the far side of the bridge separating Lake Voulismeni from the harbour (☎ 0841-22 357, fax 26 398), 8am-9.30pm from the beginning of April to mid-November. Comprehensive information about the Agios Nikolaos region, plus hotel brochures and help with reservations.

Rethymno
On the beach side of El Venizelou, opposite the junction with Kalergi (☎ 0831-29 148), Mon-Fri 8am-8pm in summer; 8am-3pm in winter. You can get a map, a bus schedule and information about local events.

Paleohora
El Venizelou, in the town hall (☎ 0823-41 507), Wed-Mon 10am-1pm & 6-9pm (May to October). You can get a map, boat schedules and a brochure about regional walks.

Tourist Police
Contact the tourist police if you think you have been ripped off by a hotel, restaurant, travel agent, tourist shop, tourist guide, waiter, taxi driver or bus driver.

Agios Nikolaos
Kontogianni 34 (☎ 0841-26 900), 7.30am-2.30pm

Hania
Irakliou 23 (☎ 0821-53 333), Mon-Fri 7.30am-2.30pm

Iraklio
Dikeosynis 10 (☎ 081-283 190), Mon-Fri 7am-11pm

Rethymno
El Venizelou, next to the tourist office (☎ 0831-28 156), 7am-10pm

Embassies

In Crete, there's only a UK consulate in Iraklio (at Apalexandrou 16, ☎ 081-22 4012). Other nationalities can contact their embassies or consulates in Athens:

Australia	☎ 644 7303
Canada	☎ 725 4011
New Zealand consulate	☎ 771 0112
South Africa	☎ 680 6645
USA	☎ 721 2951

Money

Currency
The monetary unit is the drachma (dr). Coins are for 5, 10, 20, 50 and 100 dr. Notes are for 50, 100, 200, 500, 1000, 5000 and 10,000 dr.

Travellers Cheques
The main reason to carry travellers cheques rather than cash is the protection they offer against theft. They are, however, losing popularity as more and more travellers opt to put their money in a bank at home and withdraw it at ATMs as they go along. American Express, Visa and Thomas Cook cheques are widely accepted in hotels, shops and car-rental agencies but you'll get a better rate if you change the travellers cheques into Greek drachma in a bank or exchange office.

ATMs
ATMs are found in almost every town large enough to support a bank – especially in tourist areas. If you have MasterCard, Visa, Cirrus, Plus or Maestro, there are plenty of places to withdraw money. Don't forget to get a four-digit PIN before leaving home.

Credit Cards
The main credit cards are MasterCard, Visa (Access in the UK) and Eurocard while the main charge cards are American Express and Diners Club, which are widely accepted in tourist areas but unheard of elsewhere. Most good hotels accept credit cards; some mid-range hotels will accept them, but budget hotels rarely do. Posher restaurants accept credit cards but you can forget about using them in tavernas. For lost cards contact:

American Express	☎ 1-326-2626
Diners Club	☎ 9290150
	(24 hrs, 7 days a week)
MasterCard/ Eurocard	☎ 00-800-11-887-0303
Visa	☎ 1-410-581 9 9 94

Tipping

In restaurants the service charge is included but it's the custom to leave a small amount to round up the bill. Hairdressers, porters and taxi drivers should get a few hundred dr as a tip but room cleaners are not tipped. Guides should get about 300 dr for a half-day excursion.

Discounts

Students with an International Student Identity Card (ISIC) can get a discount of about 50% on most archaeological sites and museums, and students from the EU can often get in free. Seniors over 65 may also be eligible for a 50% reduced price at many museums and archaeological sites but many of these discounts are reserved for residents of the EU.

Opening Hours

Banks
Banks are open Mon-Thurs 8am-2pm, Fri 8am-1.30pm. In big centres some banks also open Mon-Fri 3.30-6.30pm and Saturday morning.

Post Offices

Post offices open Mon-Fri 7.30am-2pm. In big cities, Mon-Fri 7.30am-8pm and Sat 7.30am-2pm.

Offices

Opening hours for offices vary widely. Theoretically they open Mon-Fri from about 8 or 9am to about 2 or 2.30pm, and they may open again later in the afternoon. If you need to get something done it's best to show up in the morning.

Shops

Most shops in tourist resorts are open 7 days a week, at least in the high season. Shops open at about 8am and may close in the afternoon, reopening at about 4 or 5pm until 8 or 9pm.

Pharmacies

Pharmacies in Crete are usually marked by a green or red cross. They are open Mon and Wed from 8am-2.30pm and Tues, Thurs and Fri from 8am-2pm & 5-8pm. If you need help with prescriptions outside of these hours go to the nearest pharmacy for a list of pharmacies on duty.

Public Holidays

New Year's Day	1 January
Epiphany	6 January
First Sunday in Lent	February
Greek Independence Day	25 March
(Orthodox) Good Friday	March/April
(Orthodox) Easter Sunday	March/April
Spring Festival/Labour Day	1 May
Feast of the Assumption	15 August
Ohi ('No') Day	28 October
Christmas Day	25 December
St Stephen's Day	26 December

All banks, shops and most museums and ancient sites close on public holidays.

Time

Greece is 2hrs ahead of Greenwich Mean Time (GMT) and 3hrs ahead from late March to late September.

At noon in Crete, it's:
 5am in San Francisco
 9am in New York
 11am in Paris
 noon in Cape Town
 8pm in Sydney

Electricity

Standard voltage is 220V, 50 Hz. Plugs are the standard continental type, with 2 round pins.

Weights & Measures

Greece uses the metric system. Liquids are often sold by weight rather than volume, eg 959g of wine is equivalent to 1 litre. Greeks indicate decimals with commas and thousands with points. See the conversion table on p. 121.

Post

The main town post offices are:

Agios Nikolaos
  28 Oktovriou 9 (3, G3); open Mon-Fri 7.30am-2pm

Hania
  Tzanakaki 3 (5, H6); open Mon-Fri 7.30am-8pm; Sat 7.30am-2pm

Iraklio
  Plateia Daskalogianni (1, F7); open Mon-Fri 7.30am-8pm; Sat 7.30am-2pm

Rethymno
  Moatsou 2 (4, K6); open Mon-Fri 7.30am-2pm

Sending Mail

Stamps are sold at post-office counters and *periptera* (kiosks), but at the latter there's a 10% surcharge. Do not wrap a parcel until it has been inspected at a post office.

Telephone

Public telephones use phonecards, which come in denominations of 100, 500 and 1000 units. A local call costs 1 unit. Get 100-unit cards from *periptera*, corner shops and tourist shops, and 500 and 1000-unit cards from OTE (Organismos Tilepikoinonion Ellados, which maintains the telephone service) offices.

Lonely Planet's eKno Communications Card, specifically aimed at travellers, provides competitive international calls (avoid using it for local calls), messaging services and free email. For free information on joining and accessing the service, visit the eKno site at www.eKno.lonelyplanet.com.

Each phone number in Greece is preceded by an area code that begins with a 0. If you're calling outside your calling area you dial the full number but if you're calling from outside Greece, dial the country code (30) followed by the digits after the 0.

Useful Numbers

Directory Inquiries	☎ 132
International Operator	☎ 161
Domestic Operator	☎ 151
International Dialling Code	☎ 00
Reverse Charge (collect)	☎ 161
Instructions for International Calls	☎ 169
Telephoned Telegrams Abroad	☎ 165

International Codes

Australia	☎ 61
Canada	☎ 1
New Zealand	☎ 64
South Africa	☎ 27
UK	☎ 44
USA	☎ 1

Email/www

Crete is not exactly leaping into cyberspace but a reliable Internet connection is possible throughout the island.

Internet Cafes

You'll find Internet cafes (see page 87) in all major cities, usually with an ISDN connection for which you'll pay about 1000 dr a half-hour.

Useful Sites

The Lonely Planet Web site (www.lonelyplanet.com) has information on Crete and Greece, as well as travel news and links to other useful travel resources. You may also find these sites useful:

www.gogreece.com
Internet guide to Greece

www.forthnet.gr/stigmes/destcret.htm
Stigmes, the magazine of Crete

www.greekislands.gr/
information about ferry schedules, car rental, hotels and flights

www.uch.gr/crete/CRETE.html
Crete information (not as good as Stigmes)

www.kriti.net
in 5 languages

www.athensnews.dolnet.gr/
web site of *Athens News*, the only daily English-language newspaper

www.Gtpnet.gr
Greek ferry schedules

www.interkriti.gr
links to hotels, apartments, shops and restaurants plus a bulletin board

www.ktel.org
maps and bus schedules

Newspapers & Magazines

The English and German newspaper, *Cretasummer*, is published monthly during the summer in Rethymno and contains Greek news, Cretan features and many ads. The monthly magazine *Kreta* is on sale in a variety of languages and contains some useful information among the ads. You may be able to pick up a copy of the English-language *Athens News* in major resorts. You'll find the *International Herald Tribune* on sale in major cities, as well as *Time*, *Newsweek* and many British daily newspapers.

Radio

If you have a short-wave radio you can access the BBC World Service for English-language news in the morning, as well as Voice of America. If you're interested in Greek or Cretan music, dial-hopping can be rewarding since stations exhibit a pronounced preference for local music.

TV

Local channels include Creta Channel, Kastro TV, Kidon TV, CreteTV, Crete 1 and Sitia TV. In addition to local, national and international news in Greek, you may find a subtitled American or British movie. Most of the better quality hotels have satellite TV where you pick up CNN.

Photography & Video

Major brands of print and slide film are widely available, although they can be expensive in small towns. Because of the brilliant sunlight in summer, you'll get better results with a polarising filter.

Greece uses the PAL video system, which is incompatible with the North American and Japanese NTSC system.

Never photograph a military installation or anything else that has a sign banning photography. You cannot photograph in muse-

ums but you can photograph archaeological sites as long as it is not for commercial purposes.

Health

Precautions
Tap water is safe to drink. You may have mild intestinal problems if you're not used to copious amounts of olive oil.

Insurance & Medical Treatment
EU nationals with an E111 form can get free treatment in public hospitals. Emergency treatment in public hospitals is free for all nationalities.

Although medical training is of a high standard, the Greek health service is one of the worst in Europe: hospitals are overcrowded, hygiene is not always reliable and relatives are expected to bring in food for the patient. Conditions and treatment are better in (expensive) private hospitals. A good travel insurance policy is essential.

Medical Services
Hospitals with 24-hour accident, emergency and dental departments include:

Apollonia Hospital
(☎ 081-22 9713), inside the old walls on Mousourou, Iraklio

General Hospital
(☎ 0821-27-000), junction of Dragoumi and Kapodistriou, Hania

Agios Nikolaos General Hospital
(☎ 0841-25 221), between Lassithiou and Paleologou, Agios Nikolaos

Rethymno General Hospital
(☎ 0831-27 814), at the corner of Trandalidou and Kriari, Rethymno

Pharmacies & Drugs
Codeine, common in headache preparations, is banned in Greece;

check labels carefully or risk prosecution. There are strict regulations about importing medicines into Greece, so bring a doctor's certificate that outlines the medication you have to take.

Pharmacies can dispense medicines which are available only on prescription in most European countries, so you can consult a pharmacist for minor ailments.

See the earlier Opening Hours section for trading hours.

HIV/AIDS

Condoms are widely available both in pharmacies and in the bathrooms of many trendy clubs, discos and bars. For an AIDS/HIV hotline call Athens at ☎ 01-722 2222.

Toilets

Public toilets are few and far between. If you're caught short, a visit to the nearest cafe is the best solution, and you usually don't need to buy anything. Next to the toilet is a wastebasket where you're expected to put the toilet paper to avoid blocking up the toilet.

Emergency Numbers

Medical Emergencies	☎ 166
Police	☎ 100
Fire	☎ 199
Tourist Police	☎ 171
Road Assistance	☎ 104

Safety Concerns

Crime, especially theft, is low in Crete. Walking around major cities at night or leaving things on the beach generally poses no problem but it would be unwise to leave valuables in an unattended car. If you encounter any violence it would likely be perpetrated by drunken youths in the resorts of Malia and Hersonisos.

Women Travellers

Many women travel alone in Greece and, as the crime rate is low, are probably safer than they would be in most European countries. Most Greek men treat foreign women with respect and are genuinely helpful. The biggest nuisance to foreign women travelling alone are the *kamakia* (see p. 91). Tampons and other feminine products are only sold in pharmacies. It should be no trouble refilling a birth-control prescription in a pharmacy or finding other contraceptives.

Gay & Lesbian Travellers

Homosexuality is generally frowned upon, especially outside the major cities. It pays to be discreet and to avoid open displays of affection. The age of consent for homosexual and heterosexual females is 15; the age of consent for homosexual men is 17 and for heterosexual men it is 16.

Information & Organisations

Check out the Roz Mov Web site at www.geocities.com/westhollywood/2225/index.html for details of gay travel info, press, organisations, events and legal issues.

Disabled Travellers

Most hotels, museums and ancient sites in Crete are not wheelchair accessible. Disabled people do come to Crete for holidays, but such a trip requires careful planning.

Information & Organisations

The British-based Royal Association for Disability and Rehabilitation (RADAR) publishes a useful guide, *Holidays & Travel Abroad: A Guide for Disabled People*, which outlines facilities for disabled travellers in Europe.

Lavinia Tours (☎ 031-23 2828, fax 031-21 9714), PO Box 111 06, Thessaloniki 541 10, specialises in arranging tours for disabled travellers. Its managing director, Eugenia Stravropoulou, has travelled widely both in Greece and abroad in her wheelchair.

Language

Greek is probably the oldest European language, with an oral tradition of 4000 years and a written tradition of about 3000 years. The modern Greek language is a southern Greek dialect which is now used by most Greek speakers in Greece and abroad. Greek is spoken throughout Greece by a population of about 10 million and by some 5 million Greeks living abroad.

English is widely spoken, especially in the major tourist centres. Younger Greeks learn English in school but older Greeks are still monolingual. You may have some trouble making yourself understood in family-run rent rooms or village tavernas but there's likely to be someone around to help you out.

The Cretan Dialect

Born of isolation, yet sharing characteristics of the dialect of Cyprus to the east, the Cretan dialect is as rugged and individualistic as its speakers.

The vernacular of Cretan villages has words unknown on the mainland, but for most observers it is the accent rather than vocabulary that distinguishes spoken Cretan from standard Greek. Spoken Cretan is characterised by its lilting softness – much like Irish English. Consonants such as 'k' become 'ch' and the gutteral 'h' becomes 'sh' or 'zh'.

The written language reached its peak during the Cretan literary renaissance of 1570-1669. In the 20th century, Cretan novelist Nikos Kazantzakis drew on the Cretan dialect for his works, which included *Zorba the Greek*.

Basics

Hello.	*Yasu* (informal)
	Yasas (polite, pl)
Goodbye.	*Andio.*
Yes/No.	*Ne/Okhi.*
Please	*Sas parakalo.*
Thank you.	*Sas efkharisto.*
You're welcome.	*Parakalo.*
Excuse me.	*Signomi.*
Do you speak English?	*Milate anglika?*
How much is it?	*Poso kani?*

Getting Around

What time does the ... leave/arrive?	*Ti ora fevyi/apo horito ...?*
boat	*to plio*
bus	*to leoforio*
tram	*to tram*
train	*to treno*
I'd like a ... ticket.	*Tha ithela isitirio ...*
one-way	*horis epistrofi*
return	*met epistrois*
left luggage	*horos aspokevon*
timetable	*dhromologhio*
bus stop	*i stasi tu leoforiu*

Around Town

a bank	*mia trapeza*
the ... embassy	*i ... presvia*
the hotel	*to ksenodho khio*
the post office	*to takhidhromio*
the market	*i aghora*
pharmacy	*farmakio*
newsagency	*efimeridhon*
the telephone centre	*to tilefoniko kentro*
the tourist office	*to ghrafio turistikon pliroforion*

Transliteration & Variant Spellings

The Greeks are not very consistent when it comes to providing transliterated names. The word 'Iraklio', for example, has been transliterated as Iraklio, Iraklion, Heraklion and Herakleion; Hania is sometimes Chania; Rethymno can be Rethimno or Rethymnon. Sometimes the letter m is dropped when it appears before another consonant; thus Tombazi becomes Tobazi and Arambatzoglou becomes Arabatzoglou. Greeks often find it unnecessary to transliterate 2 consonants when 1 will do; you may find Lasithi instead of Lassithi, Hersonisos instead of Hersonissos, and Amoudara instead of Ammoudara.

Problems in transliteration have particular implications for **vowels**, especially given that Greek has 6 ways of rendering the vowel sound *ee*, 2 ways of rendering the *o* sound and 2 ways of rendering the *e* sound. In the case of the Greek vowel combinations that make the *ee* sound, an *i* has been used in this book. For the 2 Greek *e* sounds, an *e* has been employed.

As far as **consonants** are concerned, the Greek letter *gamma* appears as *g* rather than *y* throughout this book. This means that *agios* (Greek for male saint) is used rather than *ayios*, and *agia* (Greek for female saint) rather than *ayia*. The letter *delta* appears as *d*, rather than *dh*, throughout this book (eg *dolmades* rather than *dholmades*). The letter *fi* can be transliterated as either *f* or *ph*. Here, a general rule of thumb is that classical names are spelt with a *ph* and modern names with an *f*. So Phaestos is used rather than Festos and Falassarna rather than Phalassarna. The Greek *chi* has been more or less represented as *h* in order to give as close as possible an approximation of the pronunciation of the Greek. Thus we have Hania and Hersonisos. The letter *kapa* has been used to represent that sound, except where well-known names from antiquity have adopted by convention the letter c, eg acropolis.

Where reference to **street names** are made, we have omitted the Greek word *odos*. The word for square (*plateia*) has however been included to assist in differentiating types of locations.

For a more detailed guide to the Greek language, see Lonely Planet's *Greek phrasebook*.

What time does it	*Ti ora*	tomorrow	*avrio*
open/close?	*aniyi/klini?*	yesterday	*hthes*

Accommodation		Monday	*Dheftera*
a hotel	*ena xenothohio*	Tuesday	*Triti*
a camp site	*ena kamping*	Wednesday	*Tetarti*
I'd like a ... room.	*Thelo ena*	Thursday	*Pempti*
	dhomatio ...	Friday	*Paraskevi*
single	*ya ena atomo*	Saturday	*Savato*
double	*ya dhio atoma*	Sunday	*Kiryaki*

1	*ena*	7	*epta*
How much is it ...?	*Poso kostizi ...?*		
2	*dhio*	8	*okhto*
per night	*ya ena vradhi*		
3	*tria*	9	*enea*
per person	*ya ena atomo*		
4	*tesera*	10	*dheka*
		5	*pende*	100	*ekato*

Time, Days & Numbers

What time is it?	*Ti ora ine?*	6	*eksi*	1000	*khilya*
today	*simera*		

one million   *ena ekatomirio*

Glossary

acropolis – highest point of an ancient city
agia (f), **agios** (m) – saint
agora – commercial area of an ancient city; shopping precinct in modern Greece
amphora – large vase for storing wine or oil
ANEK – Anonymi Naftiliaki Eteria Kritis; main shipping line to Crete

Byzantine Empire – named after Byzantium, the city on the Bosporus which became the capital of the Roman Empire in 324AD

capital – top of a column

delfini – dolphin; common name for hydrofoil
Dorians – Hellenic warriors who invaded Greece around 1200BC, destroying the Mycenaean civilisation and heralding Greece's 'dark age'

ELPA – Elliniki Leshi Periigiseon & Afto-kinitou; Greek motoring and touring club
EOT – Ellinikos Organismos Tourismou; national tourism organisation
estiatorio – restaurant serving ready-made food as well as à la carte dishes

frappé – iced coffee

galaktopoleio (s), **galaktopoleia** (pl) – a shop which sells dairy products
Geometric period (1200-800BC) – period characterised by pottery decorated with geometric designs; sometimes referred to as Greece's 'dark age'

Hellas, **Ellas** or **Ellada** – the Greek name for Greece
hora – main town

ikonostasis – altar screen embellished with icons

kafeneio (s), **kafeneia** (pl) – traditionally a male-only coffee house where cards and backgammon are played
KTEL – Kino Tamio Ispraxeon Leoforion; national bus cooperative that runs all long-distance bus services
Kriti – the Greek name for Crete

libations – in ancient Greece, wine or food which was offered to the gods
Linear A – Minoan script; so far undeciphered
Linear B – Mycenaean script; deciphered
lyra – small violin-like instrument

malakas – literally 'wanker'; used as a familiar term of address, or as an insult, depending on context
megaron – central room of a Mycenaean palace
meltemi – north-easterly wind which blows throug much of Greece during the summer
meze (s), **mezedes** (pl) – appetiser
Minoan civilisation (3000-1100BC) – Bronze Age culture of Crete named after the mythical King Minos and characterised by beautiful pottery and metalwork
moni – monastery or convent
Mycenaean civilisation (1900-1100BC) – first great civilisation of the Greek mainland, characterised by powerful independent city-states ruled by kings
myzithra – soft sheep's milk cheese

necropolis – literally 'city of the dead'; ancient cemetery

OA – Olympiaki Aeroporia or Olympic Airways; Greece's national airline
odeion – ancient Greek indoor theatre
odos – street
ohi – 'no'; what the Greeks said to Mussolini's ultimatum to surrender or be invaded; the Italians were subsequently repelled and the event is celebrated on October 28
OTE – Organismos Tilepikinonion Ellados; Greece's major telecommunications carrier
ouzeri (s), **ouzeria** (pl) – place which serves *ouzo* and light snacks
ouzo – a distilled spirit made from grapes and flavoured with aniseed

Panagia – Mother of God; name frequently used for churches
pantopoleio – general store
periptero (s), **periptera** (pl) – streek kiosk
pithos (s), **pithoi** (pl) – Minoan storage jar
plateia – square

rent rooms – local accommodation
retsina – resinated white wine
rhyton – another name for a libation vessel
rizitika – traditional, patriotic songs of Crete

spilia – cave

taverna – traditional restaurant which serves food and wine
tholos – Mycenaean tomb shaped like a beehive
tsikoudia – Cretan version of *tsipouro*, a distilled spirit made from grapes

xythomyzithra – soft sheep's milk cheese

zaharoplasteio (s), **zaharoplasteia** (pl) – pâtisserie; shop selling cakes, chocolates, sweets and sometimes alcoholic drinks

Conversion Table

Clothing Sizes

Measurements approximate only; try before you buy.

Women's Clothing

Aust/NZ	8	10	12	14	16	18
Europe	36	38	40	42	44	46
Japan	5	7	9	11	13	15
UK	8	10	12	14	16	18
USA	6	8	10	12	14	16

Women's Shoes

Aust/NZ	5	6	7	8	9	10
Europe	35	36	37	38	39	40
France only	35	36	38	39	40	42
Japan	22	23	24	25	26	27
UK	3½	4½	5½	6½	7½	8½
USA	5	6	7	8	9	10

Men's Clothing

Aust/NZ	92	96	100	104	108	112
Europe	46	48	50	52	54	56
Japan	S		M	M		L
UK	35	36	37	38	39	40
USA	35	36	37	38	39	40

Men's Shirts (Collar Sizes)

Aust/NZ	38	39	40	41	42	43
Europe	38	39	40	41	42	43
Japan	38	39	40	41	42	43
UK	15	15½	16	16½	17	17½
USA	15	15½	16	16½	17	17½

Men's Shoes

Aust/NZ	7	8	9	10	11	12
Europe	41	42	43	44½	46	47
Japan	26	27	27.5	28	29	30
UK	7	8	9	10	11	12
USA	7½	8½	9½	10½	11½	12½

Weights & Measures

Length & Distance

1 inch = 2.54cm
1cm = 0.39 inches
1m = 3.3ft
1ft = 0.3m
1km = 0.62 miles
1 mile = 1.6km

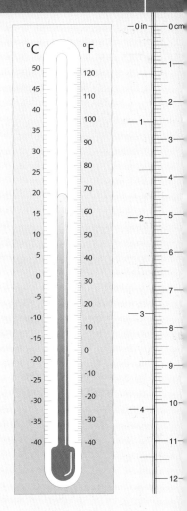

Weight

1kg = 2.2lb
1lb = 0.45kg
1g = 0.04oz
1oz = 28g

Volume

1 litre = 0.26 US gallons
1 US gallon = 3.8 litres
1 litre = 0.22 imperial gallons
1 imperial gallon = 4.55 litres

THE AUTHOR

Jeanne Oliver

Born in New Jersey, Jeanne Oliver spent her childhood mulling over the *New York Times* travel section and plotting her future voyages. After a law degree, she set up a legal practice that was interrupted by increasingly frequent trips to Central and South America, Europe and the Middle East. She moved to Paris in 1992, taught law, translated and worked in the tourist business before turning to journalism. In between magazine articles and guidebooks Jeanne vacationed on Crete, becoming ever more intrigued by the beauty of the island and its fascinating culture.

ABOUT LONELY PLANET GUIDEBOOKS

The story begins with a classic travel adventure: Tony and Maureen Wheeler's 1972 journey across Europe and Asia to Australia. Useful information about the overland trail did not exist at that time, so Tony and Maureen published the first Lonely Planet guidebook to meet a growing need.

From a kitchen table, then from a tiny office in Melbourne, Australia, Lonely Planet has become the largest independent travel publisher in the world, an international company with offices in Melbourne, Oakland (USA), London (UK) and Paris (France).

Today there are over 400 titles, including travel guides, city maps, cycling guides, first time travel guides, healthy travel guides, travel atlases, diving guides, pictorial books, phrasebooks, restaurant guides, travel literature, walking guides and world food guides.

At Lonely Planet we believe that travellers can make a positive contribution to the countries they visit – if they respect their host communities and spend their money wisely. Since 1986 a percentage of the income from books has been donated to aid projects and human rights campaigns.

ABOUT THE CONDENSED GUIDES

Other Lonely Planet Condensed guides include: *Amsterdam* (due July 2000), *California, London, New York City, Paris* and *Sydney*.

ABOUT THIS BOOK

Series developed by Diana Saad • Edited by Suzi Petkovski, with assistance from Emma Miller • Design by Andrew Weatherill • Layout by Trudi Canavan • Publishing Manager Mary Neighbour • Cover design by Indra Kilfoyle • Maps by Charles Rawlings-Way • Software engineering by Dan Levin • Thanks to Andrew Tudor, Brett Pascoe, Fiona Croyden, Gabrielle Green, Lara Morcombe, Paul Hellander, Richard I'Anson and Tim Uden

LONELY PLANET ONLINE

www.lonelyplanet.com or AOL keyword: lp
Lonely Planet's award-winning Web site has insider info on hundreds of destinations from Amsterdam to Zimbabwe, complete with interactive maps and colour photographs. You'll also find the latest travel news, recent reports from travellers on the road, guidebook upgrades and a lively bulletin board where you can meet fellow travellers, swap recommendations and seek advice.

PLANET TALK

Our FREE quarterly printed newsletter is full of tips from travellers and anecdotes from Lonely Planet authors. Every issue is packed with up-to-date travel news and advice, and includes a postcard from Lonely Planet co-founder Tony Wheeler, mail from travellers, a look at life on the road through the eyes of a Lonely Planet author, topical health advice, prizes for the best travel yarn, news about forthcoming Lonely Planet events and a complete list of Lonely Planet books and products.

To join our mailing list, email us at: go@lonelyplanet.co.uk (UK, Europe and Africa residents); info@lonelyplanet.com (North and South America residents); talk2us@lonelyplanet.com.au (the rest of the world); or contact any Lonely Planet office.

COMET

Our FREE monthly email newsletter brings you all the latest travel news, features, interviews, competitions, destination ideas, travellers' tips & tales, Q&As, raging debates and related links. Find out what's new on the Lonely Planet Web site and which books are about to hit the shelves.

Subscribe from your desktop: www.lonelyplanet.com/comet

LONELY PLANET OFFICES

Australia
PO Box 617, Hawthorn, Victoria 3122
☎ 03 9819 1877 fax 03 9819 6459
email: talk2us@lonelyplanet.com.au

USA
150 Linden St, Oakland, CA 94607
☎ 510 893 8555 TOLL FREE: 800 275 8555
fax 510 893 8572
email: info@lonelyplanet.com

UK
10a Spring Place, London NW5 3BH
☎ 020 7428 4800 fax 020 7428 4828
email: go@lonelyplanet.co.uk

France
1 rue du Dahomey, 75011 Paris
☎ 01 55 25 33 00 fax 01 55 25 33 01
email: bip@lonelyplanet.fr
minitel: 3615 lonelyplanet

World Wide Web: www.lonelyplanet.com or AOL keyword: lp
Lonely Planet Images: lpi@lonelyplanet.com.au

index

See separate indexes for Places to Eat (p. 126), Places to Stay (p. 127), Shopping (p. 127) and Sights (p.128, includes map references)

Abbreviations

AN – Agios Nikolaos
H – Hania

Ip – Ierapetra
Ir – Iraklio

R – Rethymno

A

accommodation, *see* places to stay
Agia Galini 44
Agia Roumeli 61
Agia Triada 46
Agios Nikolaos 35
    places to eat 77-8
    places to stay 98-9
    shopping 70
AIDS, *see* HIV/AIDS
air travel 109
Aktapika (Ir) 93
Angeli Café (H) 91
Anidri beach 63
Ano Viannos 50
Anogia 75
antiques 70, 71, 73
Aquarium of Agios Nikolaos 35
Archaeological Museum (AN) 35
Archaeological Museum (H) 36
Archaeological Museum (Ip) 38
Archaeological Museum (Ir) 16-17
Archaeological Museum (R) 43
Argiroupolis 18, 75
Ariadne (H) 91
arts 14
Astoria Cinema (Ir) 93

B

Bachalo 96
Baja (R) 95
Balí 44
Battle of Crete Museum (Ir) 40
beaches 44-5
beer 78
Bembo Fountain (Ir) 40
boat travel 67, 110-11
boating 55
books & bookshops 14, 70, 73, 74
bus travel 110

Byzantine Empire 7, 48

C

Café Crete (H) 91
Cafe du Lac (AN) 90
cafes, *see* places to eat
canoeing 55
car ferry 111
car travel, *see* driving
ceramics 71
chemists, *see* pharmacies
children 49
Church of Agia Ekaterini of Sinai (Ir) 40
Church of Panagia Kera 48
cinema 88
City Walls (Ir) 40-41
climate 108-9
Club 252 (R) 95
coffee 77
Covered Market (H) 36
craft 70, 71, 73, 74
credit cards 69, 113
cuisine, *see* places to eat
customs regulations 109-10
cycling 53

D

dance 88
De Facto (Ir) 93
Delfini (R) 95
Dikteon Cave 24, 62
Dimotikos Kipos Public Garden & Zoo 49
disabled travellers 117-18
diving 54
DNA (Ir) 94
Dorians 7
driving 108, 111-12
driving tours 64-5
    Hania to the Samaria Gorge 64
    Agios Nikolaos to Sitia 65
duty free 110
Dyo Lux (H) 91

E

economy 12
El Greco 14

Elafonisi beach 19
electricity 114
Elounda 55
email 115
embassies 113
Enplo (AN) 90
entertainment 88-96
    see also individual entries
environment 10-11
Evans, Sir Arthur 6

F

Fagotto Jazz Bar (H) 91
Falassarna 44
festivals 89, 96
Figaro (R) 95
fire brigade 117
fish, *see* seafood
Folk Museum (AN) 35
food, *see* places to eat
Fortezza (H) 91-2
Fortezza Disco (R) 95
Fougaro (Ir) 94
Four Lions (Ir) 93
Four Seasons (H) 92
Fournes 64
Frangokastello 20

G

Game, The (H) 92
gay & lesbian travellers 117
geography 10
Gortyn 21
Gournia 46
government 11
Guernica (Ir) 93
gyms 53

H

Hamezi 65
Hania 26, 36-7
    driving tour 64
    entertainment 91-2
    places to eat 79-80
    places to stay 99-101
    shopping 71-2
    walking tour 57-8
health 116-17
herbs 75

Hersonisos 34
hiking 54
Historical & Folk Art Museum (R) 43
Historical Museum of Crete (Ir) 41
history 6-9
HIV/AIDS 117
holidays, *see* public holidays
horse riding 54
hospitals 116
hotels, *see* places to stay
Hrysi Islet 44

I

Ice Factory (Ir), *see* Pagopeion
Ideon Antron (H) 92
Ideon Antron (Ir) 93
Ierapetra 38
Imbros Gorge 39
immunisations 108
insurance 108, 116
Internet cafes 87, 115
Iraklio 40-41
    entertainment 93-4
    places to eat 81-3
    places to stay 101-3
    shopping 73
Istron 65
IT Club, The 96

J

Janissaries (H) 37
Jasmin (Ir) 93
jet-skiing 55
jewellery 69, 71, 74

K

Kalamaki 44
Kato Zakros 33
Kazantzakis, Nikos 9, 41
Kidonia 37
knives 72
Knossos 22-3
    tours 66
Kouremenos beach 55
Kratitirio (Ir) 94
Kritiki Farma 49
Kritsa 42

L

Lakki 64
language 118
Lassithi Plateau 24-5
    walking tour 62
Lato 46
Laws of Gortyn 21
leather 69, 73

Limnoupolis Water Park 49
Linear B 16
Lipstick Disco (AN) 90
liquor 78
    liquor stores 72
Lissos 63
literature, *see* books & bookshops

M

magazines 115-16
Malia 34, 47
maps 56
Margarites 50, 75
Matala 45
Melidoni Cave 51
Meskla 64
Metropolis NYC (R) 95
Milia 51
Military Museum 51
Minoans 6
Minotaur 40
Mirsini 65
Mirtos 50
Mohlos 65
money 113
Moni Arkadiou 48
Moni Faneromenis 65
Moni Hrysoskalitissas 48
Moni Preveli 27
Moni Toplou 28
moped 111-12
Morosini Fountain (Ir) 41
Mosque of the Janissaries (H) 36
motorcycle travel, *see* driving
mountain-biking 53
music 88
    music shops 70, 72, 74
    recorded music 69
Mycenaeans 7
myths 7

N

Naval Museum (H) 37
New York Music Pub 96
newspapers 115-16
Nikos Kazantzakis Open Air Theatre (Ir) 94
Nitro Club (R) 95
Nostos Night Club 96
Notes (R) 95

O

Old Town (Ip) 38
olive oil 85
Omalos 50
opening hours 69, 113-14
Ottoman Empire 8

ouzo 78

P

Pagopeion (Ir) 93
Pahia Ammos 65
Paleohora 45, 63
Paleohora Club 96
parasailing 55
Pendlebury, John 62
pension, *see* places to stay
Phaestos 29
Phaestos disc 16, 29
pharmacies 116-17
photography 116
places to eat 76-87
    see also Places to Eat Index 126
places to stay 97-106
    see also Places to Stay Index 127
Plakias 45
Platanos 65
Point Music Bar (H) 92
police 117
Politia (Ir) 94
politics 11
Polyrrinia 47
postal services 114
Prevelakis, Pandelis 43
Preveli beach 27
Privilege Club (Ir) 94
public holidays 114

R

radio 116
raki 78
resorts, *see* places to stay
restaurants, *see* places to eat
Rethymno 30, 43
    entertainment 95
    places to eat 84-5
    places to stay 103-5
    shopping 74
Rethymno beach 43
retsina 78
Rex 'Polycenter' (AN) 90
Rififi (AN) 90
Rimondi Fountain 30
Rocca al Mare Fortress (Ir) 41
Roman Empire 7
Royale Bar (AN) 90
Rudi's Bierhaus (H) 92

S

safety 117
Samaria Gorge 31
    hiking tour 61
    tours 66
Santa Maria (AN) 90

seafood 76
Sendoni Cave 52
shopping 68-75
see also Shopping
Index 127
Silo Club (Ir) 94
Sitia 32, 75
driving tour 65
snorkelling 54
Sougia 63
Sousouro (Ir) 94
Spili 50
Spinalonga Island 52
Splendid Cocktail & Dancing
Bar 96
sport 53-5
Street Club (H) 92
Sweetwater 45
swimming 55
Synagogi (H) 92

T

Take Five (Ir) 94
tax 69, 110
taxi 110
tea 77
telephone 115
television 116
Temple of Anemospilia 52

Temple of the Pythian
Apollo 21
Thrapsano 75
time 114
tipping 113
toilets 117
Tomb of Nikos Kazantzakis
(Ir) 41
tourist information
abroad 108
in Crete 112
tourist police 112
tours 66-7
Trapeza (R) 95
travellers cheques 113
turtles 10

U

Utopia 96

V

Vaï 45
vampires 52
Vareladiko (Ir) 94
VAT 69
Venetian Empire 7-8, 48
Venetian Fortress (Ip) 38
video 116

Voulismeni Lake (AN) 35

W

walks 57-63
Hania's Old Quarter 57-8
Iraklio Stroll 59-60
Samaria Gorge Hike 61
Lassithi Plateau Walk 62
Paleohora-Sougia Coastal
Walk 63
water 77
Water City 49
waterskiing 55
weather, *see* climate
windsurfing 55
wine 75, 78
women travellers 117

X

Xerokambos 50

Y

Yacht Club (Ir) 94

Z

Zakros Palace 33
Zaros 50

PLACES TO EAT

Adiexodo (H) 79
Aithrion (Ir) 81
Akrogiali (H) 79
Anaplous (H) 79
Aouas Taverna (AN) 77
Avli (AN) 77
Avli (R) 84
Balcony, The 87
Baxes (Ir) 81
Bella Casa (Ir) 81
Cafe Eaterie Ekstra (H) 79
Doloma Restaurant (H) 79
Elā (H) 79
Embassy Garden Restaurant
(AN) 77
Estiatoria 82
Famagousta (R) 84
Fanari (R) 84
Garden of Deykaliola Taverna
(Ir) 81
Giakoumis (Ir) 81
Giovanni Taverna (Ir) 82
Gounakis Restaurant & Bar (R)
84, 95
Grammeno 86
Hippopotamus (H) 79
Ippokampos Ouzeri (Ir) 82

Istos Cyber Cafe 87
Kafeneia 82
Kariatis (H) 80
Katofli (H) 80
Katsina Ouzeri (Ir) 82
Kombos 86
Loukoulos (Ir) 82
Loukoumades (Ir) 82
Mano Café (H) 80
Mezedes 79
Mihalis 86
Mylos 86
Mystical View
Restaurant 86
Napoleon 87
Net c@fe 87
New China (Ir) 83
New Kow Loon (AN) 77
O Psaras (R) 84
Old Town Taverna (R) 84
Ouzeria 82
Pelagos (AN) 77
Polychoros 87
Restaurant du Lac (AN) 78
Restaurant Ionia (Ir) 83
Sarri's (AN) 78
Steki 87

Stella's Kitchen (R) 84
Suki Yaki (H) 80
Sunset (R) 85
Ta Leontaria (Ir) 83
Tamam (H) 80
Taverna 82
Taverna Stratidakis 87
Taverna Diktina 86
Taverna Itanos (AN) 78
Taverna Kastella (Ir) 83
Taverna Kastro (R) 85
Taverna Kyria Maria (R) 85
Taverna Nikitas 87
Taverna Pine Tree (AN) 78
Taverna Pontios (R) 85
Taverna Zisis (R) 85
Third Eye, The 86
Tholos (H) 80
Tierra del Fuego (Ir) 83
To Karnagio (H) 80
Tsikoydadiko (H) 80
Vareladika Ouzeri (Ir) 83
Votomos 87
Vranas Studios 87
Well of the Turk Restaurant &
Bar (H) 80
Zaharoplasteia 82

PLACES TO STAY

Akasti (H) 99
Amfora Hotel (H) 99
Astali (R) 103
Astoria Hotel (Ir) 101
Atlantis Hotel (Ir) 101
Atrion Hotel (Ir) 101
Casa Delfino (H) 99
Danaos (H) 100
El Greco (Ir) 101
Elena (AN) 98
Elounda Beach Hotel & Villas
    (Elounda) 105
Galaxy Hotel (Ir) 102
Grecotel Agapi Beach
    (Ammoudara) 105
Grecotel Creta Palace (R) 103
Hotel Apollon (AN) 98
Hotal Coral (AN) 98
Hotel Dias (AN) 98
Hotel Doxa (AN) 98
Hotel Fortezza (R) 103
Hotel Ideon (R) 103

Hotel Idi (Zaros) 105-6
Hotel Ilaira (Ir) 102
Hotel Irini (Ir) 102
Hotel Kastro (Ir) 102
Hotel Kronos (Ir) 102
Hotel Lato (Ir) 102
Hotel Mariella (AN) 98
Hotel Mirabello (Ir) 103
Hotel Panorama (AN) 98
Hotel Veneto (R) 103
Itanos Hotel (Karamanli)
    106
Kastelli (H) 100
Katerina Pension (AN) 98-9
Komis Studios (Keratokambos)
    106
Kydon Hotel (H) 100
Kyma Beach (R) 104
Lefteris Papadakis Rooms (R)
    104
Minos Beach Hotel &
    Bungalows (AN) 99

Miramare Hotel (AN) 99
Monastiri Pension (H) 100
Nostos Pension (H) 100
Olympic (Ir) 103
Oriental Bay Rooms
    (Paleohora) 106
Palazzo Hotel (H) 100
Park Hotel (R) 104
Pension Nora (H) 100
Pension Theresa (H) 100
Petra Mare Hotel (Ip) 106
Porto Veneziano (H) 100-101
Rent Rooms Garden (R) 104
Rent Rooms Sea View (R)
    104
Rooms for Rent Anda (R)
    104-5
Rooms to Rent Barbara
    Dolomaki (R) 105
Royal Mare Village
    (Hersonisos) 106
Vranas Studios (H) 101

SHOPPING

Aerakis (Ir) 73
Anna Karteri (AN) 70
Antiques Gallery (H) 71
Apostolos Pahtikos (H) 71
Carmela's Ceramic Shop
    (H) 71
Dorcas (Ir) 73
Georgios Chaicalis Bookshop
    (H) 72
Giorgios Galerakis (R) 74
Hania District Association of
    Handicrafts Showroom 71

Ilias Spontidakis (R) 74
International Press Bookshop
    (R) 74
Katerina Karaoglani (R) 74
Kerazoza (AN) 70
Lappa Avocado 75
Maria Patsaki (AN) 70
Melissa (R) 74
Mount Athos (H) 71
Octapous (Ir) 73
Oinohoos (H) 72
Panagiotis Eydaimon Music

Formula (AN) 70
Planet International (Ir) 73
Roka Carpets (H) 72
Spyros Valergos (Ir) 73
Studio 2000 (H) 72
Top Hanas Carpet Shop (H) 72
Tsihlakis (Ir) 73
Union of Agricultural
    Cooperatives of Sitia 75
Xenia (R) 74
Zaharias Theodorakis'
    Workshop (R) 74

sights index

Abbreviations
AN – Agios Nikolaos
H – Hania

Ir – Iraklio
R – Rethymno

Agia Galini p. 44 (2, F7)
Agia Roumeli p. 61 (2, E4)
Agia Triada p. 46 (2, F8)
Agios Markos Church (Ir) p. 40, 59 (1, E6)
Agios Minos Cathedral (Ir) p. 60 (1, F3)
Agios Nikolaos p. 35 (3)
Agios Nikolaos Church (H) p. 58 (5, F7)
Agios Titos (Ir) p. 59 (1, D7)
Anogia p. 75 (2, E8)
Ano Viannos p. 50 (2, F11)
Aquarium of Agios Nikolaos p. 35 (3, D1)
Archaeological Museum (AN) p. 35 (3, E1)
Archaeological Museum (H) p. 36 (5, F4)
Archaeological Museum (Ir) p. 16 (1, E9)
Archaeological Museum (R) p. 43 (4, E4)
Argiroupolis p. 18 (2, E5)
Bali p. 44 (2, D7)
Battle of Crete Museum (Ir) p. 40 (1, E9)
Bembo Fountain (Ir) p. 40 (1, G6)
Church of Agia Ekaterini of
  Sinai (Ir) p. 40 (1, F4)
Covered Market (H) p. 36 (5, G6)
Dikteon Cave p. 24, 62 (2, E11)
Dimotikos Kipos Public Garden p. 49 (5, J9)
Elafonisi Beach p. 19 (2, E2)
Falassarna p. 44 (2, D2)
Folk Museum (AN) p. 35 (3, G3)
Folklore Museum (H) p. 57 (5, G4)
Fournes p. 64 (2, D3)
Frangokastello p. 20 (2, F5)
Gortyn p. 21 (2, F8)
Gournia p. 46, 65 (2, E12)
Hamezi p. 65 (2, E13)
Hania p. 36 (5)
Hania's Old Quarter p. 26, 57 (5)
Hersonisos p. 34 (2, D10)
Historical & Folk Art
  Museum (R) p. 43 (4, G4)
Historical Museum of Crete (Ir) p. 41 (1, C5)
Hrysi Islet p. 44 (2, G12)
Ierapetra p. 38 (2, F12)
Imbros p. 39 (2, E5)
Imbros Gorge p. 39 (2, E5)
Iraklio p. 40, 59 (1)
Istron p. 65 (2, E12)
Kalamaki p. 44 (2, F8)
Kato Zakros p. 33 (2, E15)
Kidonia, Ancient (site) (H) p. 37 (5, E5)
Komitades p. 39 (2, F5)
Knossos p. 22 (2, E9)
Kritsa p. 42 (2, E12)
Lakki p. 64 (2, E3)
Lassithi Plateau p. 24, 62 (2, E11)
Lato p. 46 (2, E12)
Limnoupolis (Water Park) p. 49 (2, D4)

Lissos p. 63 (2, F3)
Malia p. 34, 47 (2, E11)
Margarites p. 50, 75 (2, E7)
Matala p. 45 (2, F8)
Melidoni Cave p. 51 (2, D7)
Meskla p. 64 (2, E4)
Milia p. 51 (2, E2)
Minaret (H) p. 57 (5, G6)
Mirsini p. 65 (2, E13)
Mirtos p. 50 (2, F12)
Mohlos p. 65 (2, E13)
Moni Arkadiou p. 48 (2, E7)
Moni Faneromenis p. 65 (2, E14)
Moni Hrysoskalitissas p. 48 (2, E2)
Moni Preveli p. 27 (2, F6)
Moni Toplou p. 28 (2, D14)
Morosini Fountain (Ir) p. 41 (1, E6)
Mosque of the Janissaries (H) p. 36 (5, E4)
Mt Gingilos p. 61 (2, E3)
Naval Museum (H) p. 37 (5, D3)
Nea Hora beach p. 36 (5, E1)
Omalos p. 50 (2, E3)
Omalos Plateau p. 64 (2, E3)
Pahia Ammos p. 65 (2, E13)
Paleohora p. 45 (2, F2)
Phaestos p. 29 (2, F8)
Plakias p. 45 (2, F6)
Platanos p. 65 (2, E13)
Polyrrinia p. 47 (2, D2)
Porto Guora (R) p. 30 (4, H5)
Preveli Beach p. 27 (2, F6)
Psyhro p. 62 (2, E11)
Rethymno p. 43 (4)
Rethymno Beach p. 43 (4, H7)
Rethymno's Old Quarter p. 30 (4)
Rimondi Fountain (R) p. 30 (4, F5)
Rocca al Mare Fortress (Ir) p. 41 (1, A8)
Samaria Gorge p. 31, 61 (2, E3)
Sendoni Cave p. 52 (2, E8)
Sitia p. 32 (2, E14)
Spili p. 50 (2, E6)
Spinalonga Island p. 52 (2, D12)
Splantzia quarter (H) p. 36 (5, E7)
Sweetwater Beach p. 45 (2, F4)
Temple of Anemospilia p. 52 (2, E9)
Thrapsano p. 75 (2, E10)
Tomb of Nikos Kazantzakis (Ir) p. 41 (1, J6)
Vaï p. 45 (2, D15)
Venetian Arsenal (H) p. 58 (5, E7)
Voulismeni Lake p. 35 (3, G2)
Water City p. 49 (2, E10)
Xerokambos p. 33, 50 (2, E15)
Xyloskalo p. 64 (2, E3)
Zakros Palace p. 33 (2, E15)
Zaros p. 50 (2, F8)